Washington and his Colleagues

Roosevelt Edition
The Chronicles of America Series

Washington and his Colleagues

A Chronicle of the Rise and Fall of Federalism

Volume 14

By

Henry Jones ford

Editor
Allen Johnson

Assistant Editors
Gerhard R. Lomer
Charles W. Jeffery's

Ross & Perry, Inc.
Washington, D.C.

Copyright 1918. Yale University Press
Reprinted by Ross & Perry, Inc. 2003
© Ross & Perry, Inc. 2003 on new material. All rights reserved.

Protected under the Berne Convention.

Printed in The United States of America

Ross & Perry, Inc. Publishers
216 G St., N.E
Washington, D.C 20002
Telephone (202) 675-8300
Facsimile (202) 675-8400
info@RossPerry.com

SAN 253-8555

Library of Congress Control Number. 2003100634
http://www.rossperry.com

ISBN 1-932109-14-5

Book Cover designed by Sapna. sapna@rossperry.com

☉ The paper used in this publication meets the requirements for permanence
established by the American National Standard for Information Sciences
"Permanence of Paper for Printed Library Materials" (ANSI Z39.48-1984).

All rights reserved. No copyrighted part of this publication may be reproduced,
stored in a retrieval system, or transmitted, in any form or by any means,
electronic, photocopying, recording, or otherwise, without the prior written
permission of the publisher.

WASHINGTON'S SECOND INAUGURATION, CONGRESS HALL, PHILADELPHIA, 1793

From the painting by Ferris. In the Ferris Collection of American Historical Paintings

Copyright, J L. G. Ferris

CONTENTS

I.	AN IMITATION COURT	Page 1
II.	GREAT DECISIONS	" 26
III.	THE MASTER BUILDER	" 54
IV.	ALARUMS AND EXCURSIONS	" 80
V.	TRIBUTE TO THE ALGERINES	" 104
VI.	FRENCH DESIGNS ON AMERICA	" 115
VII.	A SETTLEMENT WITH ENGLAND	" 147
VIII.	PARTY VIOLENCE	" 164
IX.	THE PERSONAL RULE OF JOHN ADAMS	" 195
	BIBLIOGRAPHICAL NOTE	" 227
	INDEX	" 231

ILLUSTRATION

WASHINGTON'S SECOND INAUGURA-
TION, CONGRESS HALL, PHILA-
DELPHIA, 1793
    From the painting by Ferris. In the
Ferris Collection of American Historical
Paintings. Copyright, J. L. G. Ferris.   *Frontispiece*

WASHINGTON AND HIS COLLEAGUES

CHAPTER I

AN IMITATION COURT

WASHINGTON was glad to remain at Mount Vernon as long as possible after he had consented to serve as President, enjoying the life of a country gentleman, which was now much more suited to his taste than official employment. He was weary of public duties and the heavy demands upon his time which had left him with little leisure for his private life at home. His correspondence during this period gives ample evidence of his extreme reluctance to reassume public responsibilities. To bring the matter to its true proportions, it must be remembered that to the view of the times the new constitution was but the latest attempt to tinker the federal scheme, and it was yet to be seen whether this endeavor would be any more successful than previous efforts had been. As for the title of President, it had already been borne by a number of congressional politicians and had been rather tarnished by the behavior of some of them. Washington was not at all eager to move in the matter before he had to, and he therefore remained on his farm until Congress met, formally declared the result of the election, and sent a committee to Mount Vernon to give him official notice. It was not until April 30, 1789, that he was formally installed as President.

Madison and Hamilton were meanwhile going ahead with their plans. This time was perhaps the happiest in their lives. They had stood together in years of struggle to start the movement for a new constitution, to steer it through the convention, and to force it on the States. Although the fight had been a long and a hard one, and although they had not won all that they had wanted, it was nevertheless a great satisfaction that they had accomplished so much, and they were now applying themselves with great zest to the organization of the new government. Madison was a member of Congress; Hamilton lived

AN IMITATION COURT

near the place where Congress held its sittings in New York and his house was a rendezvous for the federal leaders. Thither Madison would often go to talk over plans and prospects. A lady who lived near by has related how she often saw them walking and talking together, stopping sometimes to have fun with a monkey skipping about in a neighbor's yard.

At that time Madison was thirty-eight; Hamilton was thirty-two. They were little men, of the quick, dapper type. Madison was five feet six and a quarter inches tall, slim and delicate in physique, with a pale student's face lit up by bright hazel eyes. He was as plain as a Quaker in his style of dress, and his hair, which was light in color, was brushed straight back and gathered into a small queue, tied with a plain ribbon. Hamilton was of about the same stature, but his figure had wiry strength. His Scottish ancestry was manifest in his ruddy complexion and in the modeling of his features. He was more elegant than Madison in his habitual attire. He had a very erect, dignified bearing; his expression was rather severe when his features were in repose, but he had a smile of flashing radiance when he was pleased and interested. Washington, who stood over six feet two inches in his buckled shoes, had to look down over his nose when he met the young statesmen who had been the wheel horses of the federal movement.

Soon after Washington arrived in New York he sought Hamilton's aid in the management of the national finances. There was the rock on which the government of the Confederation had foundered. There the most skillful pilotage was required if the new government was to make a safe voyage. Washington's first thought had been to get Robert Morris to take charge again of the department that he had formerly managed with conspicuous ability, and while stopping in Philadelphia on his way to New York, he had approached Morris on the subject. Morris, who was now engaged in grand projects which were eventually to bring him to a debtor's prison, declined the position but strongly recommended Hamilton. This suggestion proved very acceptable to Washington, who was well aware of Hamilton's capacity.

The thorny question of etiquette was the next matter to receive Washington's attention. Personally he favored the easy hospitality to which he was accustomed in Virginia, but he knew quite well that his own taste ought not to be decisive.

AN IMITATION COURT

The forms that he might adopt would become precedents, and hence action should be taken cautiously. Washington was a methodical man. He had a well-balanced nature which was never disturbed by timidity of any kind and rarely by anxiety. His anger was strong when it was excited, but his ordinary disposition was one of massive equanimity. He was not imaginative, but he took things as they came, and did what the occasion demanded. In crises that did not admit of deliberation, his instinctive courage guided his behavior, but such crises belong to military experience, and in civil life careful deliberation was his rule. It was his practice to read important documents pen in hand to note the points. From one of his familiar letters to General Knox we learn that on rising in the morning he would turn over in his mind the day's work and would consider how to deal with it. His new circumstances soon apprised him that the first thing to be settled was his deportment as President. Under any form of government the man who is head of the state is forced, as part of his public service, to submit to public exhibition and to be exact in social observance; but, unless precautions are taken, engagements will consume his time and strength. Writing to a friend about the situation in which he found himself, Washington declared: "By the time I had done breakfast, and thence till dinner, and afterwards till bed-time, I could not get relieved from the ceremony of one visit, before I had to attend to another. In a word, I had no leisure to read or answer the dispatches that were pouring in upon me from all quarters."

The radical treatment which the situation called for was aided by a general feeling in Congress that arrangements should be made for the President different from those under the Articles of Confederation. It had been the practice for the President to keep open house. Of this custom Washington remarked that it brought the office "in perfect contempt; for the table was considered a public one, and every person, who could get introduced, conceived that he had a right to be invited to it. This, although the table was always crowded (and with mixed company, and the President considered in no better light than as a *maître d'hôtel*), was in its nature impracticable, and as many offenses given as if no table had been kept." It was important to settle the matter before Mrs. Washington joined him in New York. Inside of ten days from the time he took the oath of

AN IMITATION COURT

office, he therefore drafted a set of nine queries, copies of which he sent to Jay, Madison, Hamilton, and John Adams, with these sensible remarks:

"Many things, which appear of little importance in themselves and at the beginning, may have great and durable consequences from their having been established at the commencement of a new general government. It will be much easier to commence the Administration upon a well-adjusted system, built on tenable grounds, than to correct errors, or alter inconveniences, after they shall have been confirmed by habit. The President, in all matters of business and etiquette, can have no object but to demean himself in his public character in such a manner as to maintain the dignity of his office, without subjecting himself to the imputation of superciliousness or unnecessary reserve. Under these impressions he asks for your candid and undisguised opinion."

Only the replies of Hamilton and Adams have been preserved. Hamilton advised Washington that while "the dignity of the office should be supported , . . care will be necessary to avoid extensive disgust or discontent. . . . The notions of equality are yet, in my opinion, too general and strong to admit of such a distance being placed between the President and other branches of the Government as might even be consistent with a due proportion." Hamilton then sketched a plan for a weekly levee: "The President to accept no invitations, and to give formal entertainments only twice or four times a year, the anniversaries of important events of the Revolution." In addition, "the President on levee days, either by himself or some gentleman of his household, to give informal invitations to family dinners . . . not more than six or eight to be invited at a time, and the matter to be confined essentially to members of the legislature and other official characters. The President never to remain long at table." Hamilton observed that his views did not correspond with those of other advisers, but he urged the necessity of behaving so as "to remove the idea of too immense inequality, which I fear would excite dissatisfaction and cabal."

This was sagacious advice, and Washington would have benefited by conforming to it more closely than he did. The prevailing tenor of the advice which he received is probably reflected in the communication from Adams, who was in favor of making the government impressive through grand ceremonial. "Chamberlains, aides-

AN IMITATION COURT

de-camp, secretaries, masters of ceremonies, etc., will become necessary. . . . Neither dignity nor authority can be supported in human minds, collected into nations or any great numbers, without a splendor and majesty in some degree proportioned to them." Adams held that in no case would it be "proper for the President to make any formal public entertainment," but that this should be the function of some minister of state, although "upon such occasions the President, in his private character, might honor with his presence." The President might invite to his house in small parties what official characters or citizens of distinction he pleased, but this invitation should always be given without formality. The President should hold levees to receive "visits of compliment," and two days a week might not be too many for this purpose. The idea running through Adams's advice was that in his private character the President might live like any other private gentleman of means, but that in his public functions he should adopt a grand style. This advice, which Washington undoubtedly received from others as well as Adams, influenced Washington's behavior, and the consequences were exactly what Hamilton had predicted. According to Jefferson's recollection, many years afterward, Washington told him that General Knox and Colonel Humphreys drew up the regulations and that some were proposed "so highly strained that he absolutely rejected them." Jefferson further related that, when Washington was re-elected, Hamilton took the position that the parade of the previous inauguration ought not to be repeated, remarking that "there was too much ceremony for the character of our government."

It is a well-known characteristic of human nature to be touchy about such matters as these. Popular feeling about Washington's procedure was inflamed by reports of the grand titles which Congress was arranging to bestow upon the President. That matter was, in fact, considered by the Senate on the very day of Washington's arrival in New York and before any steps could have been taken to ascertain his views. A joint committee of the two houses reported against annexing "any style or title to the respective styles or titles of office expressed in the Constitution." But a group of Senators headed by John Adams was unwilling to let the matter drop, and another Senate committee was appointed which recommended as a proper style of address

AN IMITATION COURT

"His Highness, the President of the United States of America, and Protector of their Liberties." While the Senate debated, the House acted, addressing the President in reply to his inaugural address simply as "The President of the United States." The Senate now had practically no choice but to drop the matter, but in so doing adopted a resolution that because of its desire that "a due respect for the majesty of the people of the United States may not be hazarded by singularity," the Senate was still of the opinion "that it would be proper to annex a respectable title to the office." Thus it came about that the President of the United States is distinguished by having no title. A governor may be addressed as "Your Excellency," a judge as "Your Honor," but the chief magistrate of the nation is simply "Mr. President." It was a relief to Washington when the Senate discontinued its attempt to decorate him. He wrote to a friend, "Happily this matter is now done with, I hope never to be revived."

Details of the social entanglements in which Washington was caught at the outset of his administration are generally omitted by serious historians, but whatever illustrates life and manners is not insignificant, and events of this character had, moreover, a distinct bearing on the politics of the times. The facts indicate that Washington's arrangements were somewhat encumbered by the civic ambition of New York. That bustling town of 30,000 population desired to be the capital of the nation, and, in the splendid exertions which it made, it went rather too far. Federal Hall, designed as a City Hall, was built in part for the accommodation of Congress, on the site in Wall Street now in part occupied by the United States Sub-Treasury. The plans were made by Major Pierre Charles l'Enfant, a French engineer who had served with distinction in the Continental Army but whose clearest title to fame is the work which he did in laying out the city of Washington when it was made the national capital. Federal Hall exceeded in dignified proportions and in artistic design any public building then existing in America. The painted ceilings, the crimson damask canopies and hangings, and the handsome furniture were considered by many political agitators to be a great violation of republican simplicity. The architect was first censured in the public press and then, because of disputes, received no pay for his time and trouble, although, had he accepted a grant of city lots offered by the town council he would have

AN IMITATION COURT 13

received a compensation that would have turned out to be very valuable.

Federal Hall had been completed and presented to Congress before Washington started for New York. The local arrangements for his reception were upon a corresponding scale of magnificence, but with these Washington had had nothing to do. The barge in which he was conveyed from the Jersey shore to New York was fifty feet long, hung with red curtains and having an awning of satin. It was rowed by thirteen oarsmen, in white with blue ribbons. In the inauguration ceremonies Washington's coach was drawn by four horses with gay trappings and hoofs blackened and polished. This became his usual style. He seldom walked in the street, for he was so much a public show that that might have been attended by annoying practical inconvenience; but when he rode out with Mrs. Washington his carriage was drawn by four — sometimes six — horses, with two outriders, in livery, with powdered hair and cockades in their hats. When he rode on horseback, which he often did for exercise, he was attended by outriders and accompanied by one or more of the gentlemen of his household. Toward the end of the year there arrived from England the state coach which he used in formal visits to Congress and for other ceremonious events. It was a canary-colored chariot, decorated with gilded nymphs and cupids, and emblazoned with the Washington arms. His state was simplified when he went to church, which he did regularly every Sunday; then his coach was drawn by two horses, with two footmen behind, and was followed by a post-chaise carrying two gentlemen of his household. Washington was fond of horses and was in the habit of keeping a fine stable. The term "muslin horses" was commonly used to denote the care taken in grooming. The head groom would test the work of the stable-boys by applying a clean muslin handkerchief to the coats of the animals, and, if any stain of dirt showed, there was trouble. The night before the white horses which Washington used as President were to be taken out, their coats were covered by a paste of whiting, and the animals were swathed in wrappings. In the morning the paste was dry and with rubbing gave a marble gloss to the horses' coats. The hoofs were then blackened and polished, and even the animals' teeth were scoured. Such arrangements, however, were not peculiar to Washington's stable. This was the usual way

AN IMITATION COURT

in which grooming for "the quality" was done in that period.

The first house occupied by Washington was at the corner of Pearl and Cherry streets, then a fashionable locality. What the New York end of the Brooklyn Bridge has left of it is now known as Franklin Square. The house was so small that three of his secretaries had to lodge in one room; and Custis in his Recollections tells how one of them, who fancied he could write poetry, would sometimes disturb the others by walking the floor in his nightgown trying the rhythm of his lines by rehearsing them with loud emphasis. About a year later Washington removed to a larger house on the west side of Broadway near Bowling Green. Both buildings went down at an early date before the continual march of improvement in New York. In Washington's time Wall Street was superseding Pearl Street as the principal haunt of fashion. Here lived Alexander Hamilton and other New Yorkers prominent in their day; here were fashionable boarding-houses at which lived the leading members of Congress. When some fashionable reception was taking place, the street was gay with coaches and sedan-chairs, and the attire of the people who then gathered was as brilliant as a flight of cockatoos. It was a period of spectacular dress and behavior for both men and women, the men rivaling the women in their use of lace, silk, and satin. Dr. John Bard, the fashionable doctor of his day, who attended Washington through the severe illness which laid him up for six weeks early in his administration, habitually wore a cocked hat and a scarlet coat, his hands resting upon a massive cane as he drove about in a pony-phaeton. The scarlet waistcoat with large bright buttons which Jefferson wore on fine occasions, when he arrived on the scene, showed that he was not then averse to gay raiment. Plain styles of dress were among the many social changes ushered in by the French Revolution and the war cycle that ensued from it.

Titles figured considerably in colonial society, and the Revolutionary War did not destroy the continuity of usage. It was quite in accord with the fashion of the times that the courtesy title of Lady Washington was commonly employed in talk about the President's household. Mrs. Washington arrived in New York from Mount Vernon on May 27, 1789. She was met by the President with his barge on the Jersey shore, and as the barge passed the Battery a salute of thirteen cannon was fired. At the landing-place a large company was gathered, and the coach that took her to her home was escorted with military parade. The questions of etiquette had been settled by that time, and she performed her social duties with the ease of a Virginia gentlewoman always used to good society. She found them irksome, however, as such things had long since lost their novelty. Writing to a friend she said, "I think I am more like a state prisoner than anything else." She was then a grandmother through her children by her first husband. Although she preferred plain attire, she is described on one occasion as wearing a velvet gown over a white satin petticoat, her hair smoothed back over a moderately high cushion. It was the fashion of the times for the ladies to tent their hair up to a great height. At one of Mrs. Washington's receptions, Miss McIvers, a New York belle, had such a towering coiffure that the feathers which surmounted it brushed a lighted chandelier and caught fire. The consequences might have been serious had the fire spread to the pomatumed structure below, but one of the President's aides sprang to the rescue and smothered the burning plumes between the palms of his hands before any harm came to the young lady.

Every Tuesday while Congress was in session Washington received visitors from three to four o'clock. These receptions were known as his levees. He is described as clad in black velvet; his hair was powdered and gathered behind in a silk bag; he wore knee and shoe buckles and yellow gloves; he held a cocked hat with a cockade and a black feather edging; and he carried a long sword in a scabbard of white polished leather. As visitors were presented to him by an aide, Washington made a bow. To a candid friend who reported to him that his bows were considered to be too stiff, he replied: "Would it not have been better to throw the veil of charity over them, ascribing their stiffness to the effects of age, or to the unskillfulness of my teacher, rather than to pride and dignity of office, which God knows has no charm for me?" Washington bore with remarkable humility the criticisms of his manners that occasionally reached him.

On Friday evenings Mrs. Washington received, and these affairs were known as her "drawing-rooms." They were over by nine o'clock which was bed-time in the Washington household; for

Washington was an early riser, often getting up at four in the morning to start the day's work betimes. The "drawing-rooms" were more cheery affairs than the levees, as Mrs. Washington had simple unaffected manners, and the General had made it known that on these occasions he desired to be regarded not as the President but simply as a private gentleman. This gave him an opportunity such as he did not have at the levees to unbend and to enjoy himself. Besides these receptions a series of formal dinners was given to diplomatic representatives, high officers of government, and members of Congress. Senator Maclay of Pennsylvania recorded in the diary he kept during the First Congress that Washington would drink wine with every one in the company, addressing each in turn by name. Maclay thought it of sufficient interest to record that on one occasion a trifle was served which had been made with rancid cream. All the ladies watched to see what Mrs. Washington would do with her portion; and next day there were tittering remarks all through the fashionable part of the town over the fact that she had martyred herself and swallowed the dose. Incidentally Maclay, who was in nearly everything a vehement opponent of the policy of the Administration,

20 WASHINGTON AND HIS COLLEAGUES

bore witness to Washington's perfect courtesy. Maclay noted that in spite of his antagonistic attitude Washington invited him to dinner and paid him "marked attention," although "he knows enough to satisfy him that I will not be Senator after the 3d of March, and to the score of his good nature must I place these attentions."

In his relations with Congress, Washington followed precedents derived from the English constitutional system under which he had been educated. No question was raised by anybody at first as to the propriety of a course with which the public men of the day were familiar. He opened the session with an address to Congress couched somewhat in the style of the speech from the throne. At the first session there was talk of providing some sort of throne for him; but the proposal came to nothing. He spoke from the Vice-President's chair, and the Representatives went into the Senate chamber to hear him, as the Commons proceed to the House of Lords on such occasions. Congress, too, conformed to English precedents by voting addresses in reply, and then the members repaired to the President's "audience chamber," where the presiding officers of the two houses delivered their addresses and

AN IMITATION COURT 21

received the President's acknowledgments. These were disagreeable duties for Washington, although he discharged them conscientiously. Maclay has recorded in his diary the fact that when Washington made his first address to Congress he was "agitated and embarrassed more than ever he was by the leveled cannon or pointed musket."

It was not until June 8 that Washington settled these delicate affairs of official etiquette sufficiently to enable him to attend to details of administration. The government, although bankrupt, was in active operation, and the several executive departments were under secretaries appointed by the old Congress. The distinguished New York jurist, John Jay, now forty-four years old, had been Secretary of Foreign Affairs since 1784. He had long possessed Washington's confidence, and now retained his Secretaryship until the government was organized, whereupon he left that post to become the first chief-justice of the United States. Henry Knox of Massachusetts, aged thirty-nine, had been Secretary of War since 1785, a position to which Washington helped him. They were old friends, for Knox had served through the war with Washington in special charge of artillery. The Postmaster-General, Ebenezer

Hazard, was not in Washington's favor. While the struggle over the adoption of the Constitution was going on Hazard put a stop to the customary practice by which newspaper publishers were allowed to exchange copies by mail. Washington wrote an indignant letter to John Jay about this action which was doing mischief by "inducing a belief that the suppression of intelligence at that critical juncture was a wicked trick of policy contrived by an aristocratic junto." As soon as Washington could move in the matter, Hazard was superseded by Samuel Osgood, who as a member of the old Congress had served on a committee to examine the post-office accounts. There was no Secretary of the Treasury at that time, but the affairs of that department were in the hands of a board of commissioners,—this same Samuel Osgood, together with Walter Livingston and Arthur Lee. To all these officials Washington now applied for a written account of "the real situation" of their departments.

Several months elapsed before he was in a position to make new arrangements. The salary bill was approved September 2, 1789, and on the same day Washington commissioned Hamilton as Secretary of the Treasury, — the first of the new appointments, although in the creative enactments the Treasury Department came last. Next came Henry Knox, Secretary of War and of the Navy, on September 12; Thomas Jefferson, Secretary of State; and Edmund Randolph, Attorney-General, on September 26, on which date Osgood was also appointed. What may be said to be Washington's Cabinet was thus established, but the term itself did not come into use until 1793. At the outset no more was decided than that the new government should have executive departments, and in superficial appearance these were much like those of the old government. The Constitution made no distinct provision for a cabinet, and the only clause referring to the subject is the provision authorizing the President to "require the opinion, in writing, of the principal officer in each of the executive departments, upon any subject relating to the duties of their respective offices." This provision does not contemplate a body that should be consultative by its normal character. The prevailing opinion at the time the Constitution was framed was that the consultative function would be exercised by the Senate, which together with the President would form the Administration. Upon

24 WASHINGTON AND HIS COLLEAGUES

this ground, Mason of Virginia refused to sign the report of the constitutional convention. It was owing to practical experience and not to the language of the Constitution that the President was soon repelled from using the Senate as his privy council and was thrown back upon the aid of the heads of the executive departments, who were thus drawn close to him as his Cabinet.[1]

The inchoate character of the Cabinet for a considerable period explains what might otherwise seem to be an anomaly, — the delay of Jefferson in occupying his post. He did not arrive until March 21, 1790, when Washington had been in office nearly a year. But this situation occasioned no remark. The notion that the heads of the departments formed a cabinet, taking office with the President and reflecting his personal choice as his advisers, was not developed until long after Washington's administration, although the Cabinet itself, as a distinct feature of the system of government, dates from his first term. The importance which the Cabinet soon acquired is

[1] In this formative process the Postmaster-General was left outside in Washington's time, since his functions were purely of a business nature, not directly affected by the issues on which Washington desired advice. The Postmaster-General did not become a member of the Cabinet until 1829.

AN IMITATION COURT

evidence that, even under a written constitution, institutions owe more to circumstances than to intentions. The Constitution of the United States is no exception to the rule that the true constitution of a country is the actual distribution of power, written provisions being efficacious only in the way and to the extent that they affect such distribution in practice. Hence results may differ widely from the expectations with which those provisions are introduced. A constitution is essentially a growth and never merely a contrivance.

CHAPTER II

GREAT DECISIONS

WHILE Washington was bearing with military fortitude the rigors and annoyances of the imitation court in which he was confined, Congress reached decisions that had a vast effect in determining the actual character of the government. The first business in order of course was the raising of revenue, for the treasury was empty, and payments of interest due on the French and Spanish loans were years behind. Madison attacked this problem before Washington arrived in New York to take the oath of office. On April 8 he introduced in the House a resolution which aimed only at giving immediate effect to a scheme of duties and imposts that had been approved generally by the States in 1783. On the very next day debate upon this resolution began in the committee of the whole, for there was then no system of standing committees to intervene be-

GREAT DECISIONS

tween the House and its business. The debate soon broadened out far beyond the lines of the original scheme, and in it the student finds lucidly presented the issues of public policy that have accompanied tariff debates ever since.

Madison laid down the general principle that "commerce ought to be free, and labor and industry left at large to find its proper object," but suggested that it would be unwise to apply this principle without regard to particular circumstances. "Although interest will, in general, operate effectually to produce political good, yet there are causes in which certain factitious circumstances may divert it from its natural channel, or throw or retain it in an artificial one." In language which now reads like prophecy he referred to cases "where cities, companies, or opulent individuals engross the business from others, by having had an uninterrupted possession of it, or by the extent of their capitals being able to destroy a competition." The same situation could occur between nations, and had to be considered. There was some truth, he also thought, in the opinion "that each nation should have within itself the means of defense, independent of foreign supplies," but he considered that this argument had been urged beyond reason, as "there is good reason to believe that, when it becomes necessary, we may obtain supplies abroad as readily as any other nation whatsoever." He instanced as a cogent reason in favor of protective duties that, as the States had formerly the power of making regulations of trade to cherish their domestic interests, it must be presumed that, when they put the exercise of this power into other hands by adopting the Constitution, "they must have done this with the expectation that those interests would not be neglected" by Congress.

Actuated by such views, and doubtless also influenced by the great need for revenue, Madison was on the whole favorable to amendments extending the list of dutiable articles. Though there were conflicts between members from manufacturing districts and those from agricultural constituencies, and though the salt protectionists of New York had some difficulty in carrying their point, the contention did not follow sectional lines. Coal was added to the list on the motion of a member from Virginia. The duties levied were, however, very moderate, ranging from five to twelve and one-half per cent, with an exception in the case of one article that might be considered a luxury.

GREAT DECISIONS

The bill as it passed the House discriminated in favor of nations with which the United States had commercial treaties. That is to say, it favored France and Holland as against Great Britain, which had the bulk of America's foreign trade. Though Madison insisted on this provision and was supported by a large majority of the House, the Senate would not agree to it. During the early sessions of Congress the Senate met behind closed doors, a practice which it did not abandon until five years later. From the accounts of the discussion preserved in Maclay's diary it appears that there was much wrangling. Maclay relates that on one occasion when Pennsylvania's demands were sharply attacked, his colleague, Robert Morris, was so incensed that Maclay "could see his nostrils widen and his nose flatten like the head of a viper." Pierce Butler of South Carolina "flamed away and threatened a dissolution of the Union, with regard to his State, as sure as God was in the firmament." Thus began a line of argument that was frequently pursued thereafter until it was ended by wager of battle. On several occasions the division was so close that Vice-President Adams gave the casting vote. Although there was much railing in the Senate against imposts as a burden to the agricultural sections, yet some who opposed duties in the abstract thought of particulars that ought not to be neglected if the principle of protection were admitted. Duties on hemp and cotton therefore found their way into the bill through amendments voted by the Senate. Adjustment of the differences between the two houses was hindered by the resentment of the House at the removal of the treaty discrimination feature, but the Senate with characteristic address evaded the issue by promising to deal with it as a separate measure and ended by thwarting the House on that point.

On the whole, in view of the sharp differences of opinion, the action taken on the tariff was remarkably expeditious. The bill, which passed the House on May 16, was passed by the Senate on June 2, and although delay now ensued because of the conflict over the discrimination issue, the bill became law by the President's approval on July 4. This prompt conclusion in spite of closely-balanced factions becomes more intelligible when it is observed that the rules of the Senate then provided that, "in case of a debate becoming tedious, four Senators may call for the question."

Brief as was the period of consideration as compared with the practice since that day, Maclay noted indignantly that the merchants had "already added the amount of the duties to the price of their goods." so that a burden fell upon the consumers without advantage to the Treasury. Such consequence is evidence of defect in procedure which the experience of other nations has led them to correct, but which has continued to increase in the United States until it has attained monstrous proportions. Under the English budget system new imposts now take effect as soon as they are proposed by the government, the contingency of alteration in the course of enactment being provided for by return of payments made in error. The general tendency of civilized government is now strongly in favor of attaching the process of deliberation upon financial measures to the period of their administrative incubation, and of shortening the period of formal legislative consideration.

One of the tasks of Congress in its first session was to draught amendments to the Constitution. The reasons for such action were stated by Madison to be a desire to propitiate those who desired a bill of rights, and an effort to secure acceptance of the Constitution in Rhode Island and North Carolina. Promises had been made, in the course of the struggle for adoption, that this matter would be taken up, and there was a general willingness to proceed with it. Under the leadership of Madison, the House adopted seventeen amendments, which were reduced by the Senate to twelve. Of these, ten were eventually ratified and formed what is commonly known as the Bill of Rights.

Apart from this matter, the session, which lasted until September 29, was almost wholly occupied with measures to organize the new government. To understand the significance of the action taken, it should be remembered that the passions excited by the struggle over the new Constitution were still turbulent. Fisher Ames of Massachusetts, a member without previous national experience, who watched the proceedings with keen observation, early noticed the presence of a group of objectors whose motives he regarded as partly factious and partly temperamental. Writing to a friend about the character of the House, he remarked: "Three sorts of people are often troublesome: the anti-federals, who alone are weak and some of them well disposed; the dupes of local prejudices, who fear eastern influence, monopolies, and navigation acts; and lastly the violent republicans, as they think fit to style themselves, who are new lights in politics, who are more solicitous to establish, or rather to expatiate upon, some sounding principle of republicanism, than to protect property, cement the union, and perpetuate liberty." The spirit of opposition had from the first an experienced leader in Elbridge Gerry of Massachusetts. He had seen many years of service in the Continental Congress which he first entered in 1776. He was a delegate to the Philadelphia convention, in whose sessions he showed a contentious temper, and in the end refused to subscribe to the new Constitution. In the convention debates he had strongly declared himself "against letting the heads of the departments, particularly of finance, have anything to do with business connected with legislation." Defeated in the convention, Gerry was now bent upon making his ideas prevail in the organization of the government.

On May 19, the matter of the executive departments was brought up in committee of the whole by Boudinot of New Jersey. At this time it was the practice of Congress to take up matters first in committee of the whole, and, after general conclusions had been reached, to appoint a committee to prepare and bring in a bill. A warm discussion ensued on the question whether the heads of the departments should be removable by the President. Gerry, who did not take a prominent part in the debate, spoke with a mildness that was in marked contrast with the excitement shown by some of the speakers. He was in favor of supporting the President to the utmost and of making him as responsible as possible, but since Congress had obviously no right to confer a power not authorized by the Constitution, and since the Constitution had conditioned appointments on the consent of the Senate, it followed that removals must be subject to the same condition. He spoke briefly and only once, although the debate became long and impassioned. But he was merely reserving his fire, as subsequent developments soon showed. Without a call for the ayes and nays, the question was decided in favor of declaring the power of removal to be in the President. The committee then proceeded to the consideration of the Treasury Department. Gerry at once made a plea for delay. "He thought they were hurrying on business too rapidly. Gentlemen had already committed themselves on one very important

GREAT DECISIONS

point." He "knew nothing of the system which gentlemen proposed to adopt in arranging the Treasury Department," but the fact was worth considering that "the late Congress had, on long experience, thought proper to organize the Treasury Department, in a mode different from that now proposed." He "would be glad to know what the reasons were that would induce the committee to adopt a different system from that which had been found most beneficial to the United States."

What Gerry had in view was the retention of the then existing system of Treasury management by a Board of Commissioners. In 1781 the Continental Congress had been forced to let the Treasury pass out of its own hands into those of a Superintendent of Finance, through sheer inability to get any funds unless the change was made. Robert Morris, who held the position, had resigned in January, 1783, because of the behavior of Congress, but the attitude of the army had become so menacing that he was implored to remain in office and attend to the arrears of military pay. He had managed to effect a settlement, and at length retired from office on November 1, 1784. Congress then put the Treasury in the hands of three commissioners appointed and supervised by it. Gerry was now striving to continue this arrangement with as little change as possible.

When debate was resumed the next day, Gerry made a long, smooth speech on the many superior advantages of the Board system. The extent and variety of the functions of the office would be a trial to any one man's integrity. "Admit these innumerable opportunities for defrauding the revenue, without check or control, and it is next to impossible he should remain unsullied in reputation, or innoxious with respect to misapplying his trust." The situation would be "very disagreeable to the person appointed, provided he is an honest, upright man; it will be disagreeable also to the people of the Union, who will always have reason to suspect" misconduct. "We have had a Board of Treasury and we have had a Financier. Have not express charges, as well as vague rumors, been brought against him at the bar of the public? They may be unfounded, it is true; but it shows that a man cannot serve in such a station without exciting popular clamor. It is very well known, I dare say, to many gentlemen in this House, that the noise and commotion were such as obliged Congress once more to alter their Treasury Department, and place it under the management of a Board of

Commissioners." He descanted upon the perils to liberty involved in the course they were pursuing. Surround the President with Ministers of State and "the President will be induced to place more confidence in them than in the Senate. . . . An oligarchy will be confirmed upon the ruin of the democracy; a government most hateful will descend to our posterity and all our exertions in the glorious cause of freedom will be frustrated."

Gerry's speech as a whole was tactful and persuasive, but he made a blunder when he appealed to the recollections of the old members, men who had been in the Continental Congress, or else in some position where they could view its springs of action. Their recollections now came forward to his discomfiture. "My official duty," said Wadsworth of Connecticut, "has led me often to attend at the Treasury of the United States, and, from my experience, I venture to pronounce that a Board of Treasury is the worst of all institutions. They have doubled our national debt." He contrasted the order and clearness of accounts while the Superintendent of Finance was in charge with the situation since then. If the committee had before them the transactions of the Treasury Board, "instead of system and responsibility they would find nothing but confusion and disorder, without a possibility of checking their accounts." Boudinot of New Jersey said he "would state a circumstance which might give the committee some small idea of what the savings under the Superintendent were. The expenditure of hay at a certain post was one hundred and forty tons; such was the estimate laid before him; yet twelve tons carried the post through the year, and the supply was abundant, and the post was as fully and usefully occupied as it had ever been before." Of course there was an outcry against the Superintendent of Finance; "he rather wondered that the clamor was not more loud and tremendous." He remembered that "one hundred and forty-six supernumerary officers were brushed off in one day, who had long been sucking the vital blood and spirit of the nation. Was it to be wondered at, if this swarm should raise a buzz about him?" Gerry fought on almost singlehanded, but he could not refute the evidence that he had invited. He lost his temper and resorted to sarcasm. If a single head of the Treasury was so desirable, why not "have a single legislator; one man to make all the laws, the revenue laws particularly, because among many there is less responsibility, system, and energy; consequently a numerous representation in this House is an odious institution."

The case for the Treasury Board was so hopeless that nothing more was heard of it; but the battle over the removal question was renewed with added violence, when the bill for establishing the Department of Foreign Affairs came up for consideration. White of Virginia now led the attack. He had been a member of the Continental Congress from 1786 to 1788, and a member of the ratifying convention of his State. Although he voted for a provisional acceptance of the Constitution, he had supported an amendment requiring Congress to collect direct taxes or excises through State agency, which would have been in effect a return to the plan of requisitions — the bane of the Confederation. In an elaborate speech he attacked the clause giving the President power to remove from office, as an attempt to impart an authority not conferred by the Constitution, and inconsistent with the requirement that appointments should be made with the advice and consent of the Senate. The debate soon became heated. "Let us look around at this moment," said Jackson of Georgia, "and see the progress we are making toward venality and corruption. We already hear the sounding title of *Highness* and *Most Honorable* trumpeted in our ears, which, ten years since, would have exalted a man to a station as high as Haman's gibbet." Page of Virginia was ablaze with indignation. "Good God!" he exclaimed. "What, authorize in a free republic, by law, too, by your first act, the exertion of a dangerous royal prerogative in your Chief Magistrate!" Gerry, in remarks whose oblique criticism upon arrangements at the President's house was perfectly well understood, dwelt upon the possibility that the President might be guided by some other criterion than discharge of duty as the law directs. "Perhaps the officer is not good natured enough; he makes an ungraceful bow, or does it left leg foremost; this is unbecoming in a great officer at the President's levee. Now, because he is so unfortunate as not to be so good a dancer as he is a worthy officer, he must be removed." These rhetorical flourishes, which are significant of the undercurrent of sentiment, hardly do justice to the general quality of the debate which was marked by legal acuteness on both sides. Madison pressed home the sensible argument that the President could not be held to responsibility unless he could control his subordinates. "And if it should happen that the officers connect themselves with the Senate, they may mutually support each other, and for want of efficacy reduce the power of the President to a mere vapor; in which case, his responsibility would be annihilated and the expectation of it unjust."

The debate lasted for several days, but Madison won by a vote of 34 to 20 in committee, in favor of retaining the clause. On second thought, however, and probably after consultation with the little group of constructive statesmen who stood behind the scenes, he decided that it might be dangerous to allow the President's power of removal to rest upon a legislative grant that might be revoked. When the report from the committee of the whole was taken up in the House, a few days later, Benson of New York proposed that the disputed clause should be omitted and the language of the bill should be worded so as to imply that the power of removal was in the President. Madison accepted the suggestion, and the matter was thus settled. The point was covered by providing that the chief clerk of the Department should take charge "whenever the principal officer shall be removed from office by the President." The clause got through the Senate by the casting vote of the Vice-President, and a similar provision was inserted, without further contest, in all the acts creating the executive departments. It is rather striking evidence of the Utopian expectations which could then be indulged that Daniel Carroll of Maryland was persistent in urging that the existence of the office should be limited to a few years, "under a hope that a time would come when the United States would be disengaged from the necessity of supporting a Secretary of Foreign Affairs." Although Gerry and others expressed sympathy with the motion it was voted down without a division.

When the bill establishing the Treasury Department was taken up, Page of Virginia made a violent attack upon the clause authorizing the Secretary to "digest and report plans." He denounced it as "an attempt to create an undue influence" in the House. "Nor would the mischief stop here; it would establish a precedent which might be extended until we admitted all the Ministers of the government on the floor, to explain and support the plans they have digested and reported; thus laying the foundation for an aristocracy or a detestable monarchy." As a matter of fact, a precedent in favor of access to Congress already existed. The old Superintendent of Finance and the Board which succeeded him had the power now proposed for the Secretary of the Treasury. Livermore of New Hampshire, who had been a member of the Continental Congress, admitted this fact, but held that such power was not dangerous at that time since Congress then possessed both legislative and executive authority. They could abolish his plans and his office together, if they thought proper; "but we are restrained by a Senate and by the negative of the President." Gerry declared his assent to the views expressed by Page. "If the doctrine of having prime and great ministers of state was once well established, he did not doubt but that we should soon see them distinguished by a green or red ribbon, or other insignia of court favor and patronage."

The strongest argument in favor of retaining the clause referred to was made by Fisher Ames, who had begun to display the powers of clear statement and of convincing argument that soon established his supremacy in debate. He brought the debate at once to its proper bearings by pointing out that there were really only two matters to be considered: whether the proposed arrangement was useful, and whether it could be safely guarded from abuse. "The Secretary is presumed to acquire the best knowledge of the subject of finance of any member of the community. Now, if this House is to act on the best knowledge of circumstances, it seems to follow logically that the House must obtain the evidence from that officer; the best way of doing this will be publicly from the officer himself, by making it his duty to furnish us with it." In one of those eloquent passages which brighten the records of debate whenever Ames spoke at any length, he pictured the difficulties that had to be surmounted. "If we consider the present situation of our finances, owing to a variety of causes, we shall no doubt perceive a great, although unavoidable confusion throughout the whole scene; it presents to the imagination a deep, dark, and dreary chaos; impossible to be reduced to order without the mind of the architect is clear and capacious, and his power commensurate to the occasion." He asked, "What improper influence could a plan reported openly and officially have on the mind of any member, more than if the scheme and information were given privately at the Secretary's office?" Merely to call for information would not be advantageous to the

House. "It will be no mark of inattention or neglect, if he take time to consider the questions you propound; but if you make it his duty to furnish you plans . . . and he neglect to perform it, his conduct or capacity is virtually impeached. This will be furnishing an additional check."

Sedgwick of Massachusetts made a strong speech to the same effect. "Make your officer responsible," he said with prophetic vision, "and the presumption is, that plans and information are properly digested; but if he can secrete himself behind the curtain, he might create a noxious influence, and not be answerable for the information he gives."

The weight of the argument was heavily on the side of the supporters of the clause, and it looked as though the group of objectors would again be beaten. But now a curious thing happened. Fitzsimmons remarked that, if he understood the objection made to the clause, "it was a jealousy arising from the power given the Secretary to report plans of revenue to the House." He suggested that "harmony might be restored by changing the word 'report' into 'prepare'." Fitzsimmons was esteemed by the House because of his zealous support of the War of Independence and also because he stood high as a successful Philadelphia merchant, but he did not, however, rank as a leader. Early in the session Ames described him as a man who "is supposed to understand trade, and he assumes some weight in such matters. He is plausible, though not over civil; is artful, has a glaring eye, a down look, speaks low, and with apparent candor and coolness." He was hardly the man to guide the House on a matter pertaining to the organization of public authority.

While the removal issue was before the House, Madison had been prominent in debate, and had spoken with great power and earnestness; but up to this time he had said nothing on the issue now pending. He now remarked that he did not believe that the danger apprehended by some really existed, but twice in his speech he admitted that "there is a small possibility, though it is but small, that an officer may derive a weight from this circumstance, and have some degree of influence upon the deliberations of the legislature." In its practical effect the speech favored the compromise which Fitzsimmons had just proposed; in fact, the only opposition to the change of phrasing now came from a few extremists who still clamored for the omission of the entire clause. The decisive effect of Madison's intervention was a natural consequence of the leadership he had held in the movement for the new Constitution and of his standing as the representative of the new Administration, of his possessing Washington's confidence and acting as his adviser. Washington, then being without a cabinet, had turned to Madison for help in discharging the duties of his office, and at Washington's written request Madison had drafted for him his replies to the addresses of the House and the Senate at the opening of the session. It was a matter of course in such circumstances that the House accepted Fitzsimmons' amendment, — "by a great majority," according to the record, — and thus the Secretary of the Treasury was shut out of the House and was condemned to work in the lobby.

The consequences of this decision have been so vast that it is worth while making an inquiry into motive, although the materials upon which judgment must rest are scant. No one can read the record of this discussion without noting that Madison's approval of the original clause was lukewarm as compared with the ardor he had shown when the question was whether Washington should be allowed to remove his subordinates. This contrast suggests that Madison's behavior was affected by fear of Hamilton's influence. Would it be prudent for him to give Hamilton the advantage of being able to appear in person before the House, and probably to supplant Madison himself as the spokesman of the Administration? Divergence between the two men had already begun in details. At the time the vote on the powers of the Secretary of the Treasury was taken, the tariff bill and the tonnage bill were still pending, and Hamilton's influence operated against Madison's views on some points. Moreover, the question of the permanent residence of the federal government was coming forward and was apparently overshadowing everything else in the minds of members. Ames several times in his correspondence at this period remarks upon Madison's timidity, which was due to his concern about Virginia State politics. Any arrangement that might enable Hamilton to cross swords with an opponent on the floor of the House could not be attractive to Madison, who was a lucid reasoner but not an impressive speaker. Hamilton was both of these, and he possessed an intellectual brilliancy which Madison lacked. Ames, who respected Madison's abilities and who regarded him as the leading member of the House, wrote that "he speaks low, his person is little and ordinary; he speaks decently as to manner, and no more; his language is very pure, perspicuous, and to the point." Why Fitzsimmons should be opposed to the appearance of the Secretary in person in the House, as had been Robert Morris's practice when he was Superintendent of Finance, is plain enough. Maclay's diary has many references to Fitzsimmons's negotiations with members on tariff rates. It was not to the advantage of private diplomacy to allow the Secretary to shape and define issues on the floor of the House. But Fitzsimmons could not have had his way about the matter without Madison's help.

Gibbon remarks that the greatest of theological controversies which racked the Roman Empire and affected the peace of millions turned on the question whether a certain word should be spelled with one diphthong or another. A like disproportion between the vastness of results and the minuteness of verbal distinction is exhibited in this decision by the House. The change of "report" into "prepare" threw up a ridge in the field of constitutional development that has affected the trend of American politics ever since. This is the

50 WASHINGTON AND HIS COLLEAGUES

explanation of a problem of comparative politics that has often excited much wondering notice: why it is that alone among modern representative assemblies the American House of Representatives tends to decline in prestige and authority. The original expectation was that the House of Representatives would take a dominant position like that of the House of Commons, but its degradation began so soon that Fisher Ames noted it as early as 1797. Writing to Hamilton he observed:

"The heads of departments are chief clerks. Instead of being the ministry, the organs of the executive power, and imparting a kind of momentum to the operation of the laws, they are precluded even from communicating with the House by reports. . . . Committees already are the Ministers and while the House indulges a jealousy of encroachment in its functions, which are properly deliberative, it does not perceive that these are impaired and nullified by the monopoly as well as the perversion of information by these committees."

Justice Story, who entered Congress in 1808 as a Jeffersonian Republican, noted the process of degradation, and in his *Commentaries* he pointed out the cause: "The Executive is compelled to resort to

GREAT DECISIONS 51

secret and unseen influences, to private interviews and private arrangements to accomplish its own appropriate purposes, instead of proposing and sustaining its own duties and measures by a bold and manly appeal to the nation in the face of its representatives."

The last of the organic acts of the session was the one establishing the judiciary. The student will be disappointed if he examines the record to note whether there was any vision of the ascendancy which the judiciary was to obtain in the development of the American constitutional system. The debates were almost wholly about the possibilities of conflict between the state and the federal courts. Although Maclay's diary gives a one-sided and distorted account of the proceedings in the Senate, the course of the debate is clear. Ellsworth of Connecticut had principal charge of the bill. At the outset Lee and Grayson of Virginia made an ineffectual effort to confine the original jurisdiction of the federal courts to cases of admiralty and maritime jurisdiction, and argued that jurisdiction over other cases involving federal law might be conferred upon state courts. This was a point on which there had been some difference of opinion between Hamilton and Madison. The former held that it was within the competency of Congress, when instituting tribunals inferior to the Supreme Court, to adopt the state courts for that purpose. Madison held that nothing less than a system of federal courts quite distinct from the state courts would satisfy the requirements of the Constitution. When the bill was taken up in the House, there was a long debate over this matter. The costly duplication of judicial establishments that has ever since existed in the United States is certainly not necessary to a federal system, but is an American peculiarity. The advocates of a unified system were hampered by the fact that this view was pressed by some in a spirit of hostility to the Constitution. The decisive argument was the untrustworthiness of the state courts. Madison urged this fact with great force and pointed out that in some of the States the courts "are so dependent on the state legislatures, that to make the federal laws dependent on them, would throw us back into all the embarrassments which characterized our former situation." Such was the low repute of the state legislatures that the only way in which this argument could be met was to argue that "Congress shall have power, in its fullest extent, to correct, reverse, or affirm, any decree of a state court." This high assertion of federal authority was made by Jackson of Georgia in the course of a long legal argument. The debate did not follow sectional lines, and in general it was not unfairly described by Maclay as a lawyer's wrangle. The bill was put into shape by the Senate, and reached the House toward the close of the session when the struggle over the site of the national capital was overshadowing everything else. It was so generally believed that nothing important could be gained by attempts at amendment that, after an airing of opinions, the House accepted the measure just as it had come from the Senate.

CHAPTER III

THE MASTER BUILDER

THE subject of national finance had long interested Hamilton. His ideas had been matured by a diligent and minute study of English precedents, and now that his opportunity had come he was ready to grasp it. Soon after he took office, the House resolved that "an adequate provision for the support of the public credit" should be made, and it directed the Secretary of the Treasury "to prepare a plan for that purpose and to report the same to the House at its next meeting." This was, in effect, a postponement until the second session of the First Congress, which began in January, 1790. In his opening address to Congress, Washington pointedly referred to the public credit resolution which he had noted "with peculiar pleasure." On the next day a letter from Hamilton was read in the House stating that he had prepared his plan and was ready to report the same to the House when they should be pleased to receive it.

This announcement brought up anew the question in what manner the Secretary should make his report. Gerry was on his feet at once with a motion that it should be made in writing. Boudinot "hoped that the Secretary of the Treasury might be permitted to make his report in person, in order to answer such inquiries as the members might be disposed to make, for it was a justifiable surmise that gentlemen would not be able clearly to comprehend so intricate a subject without oral illustration." The allusion to the intricacy of the subject had the effect of turning against the plan of oral communication some who had favored giving the Secretary the same direct access to Congress that the Superintendent of Finance had formerly enjoyed. Ames, for instance, now desired that the Secretary's communications should be in writing since "in this shape they would obtain a degree of permanency favorable to the responsibility of the officer, while, at the same time, they would be less liable to be misunderstood." Benson suggested that since the resolution of Congress had directed the Secretary to make a report, it was left to his discretion to "make it in the manner for which he is prepared." Gerry adroitly countered by saying that the resolution provided for a report. That done, it would be time enough "to give him the right to lay before them his explanations, if he thinks explanations necessary." The debate was brief and one-sided; the motion for receiving the report in writing was adopted without a division. Five days later the written report was laid before the House, but the Secretary was never accorded an opportunity to offer any personal explanations.

This masterly report, which is justly regarded as the corner-stone of American public credit, excites the admiration of the reader by the clearness of its analysis, the cogency of its argument, and the broad range of its vision. The principles of action that it embodied, however, were few and simple, chief among them being exact and punctual fulfillment of contract. "States, like individuals, who observe their engagements, are respected and trusted; while the reverse is the fate of those who pursue an opposite conduct." To discharge the principal of the public debt was of course impracticable; nor was it desirable, as the creditors would be well pleased to leave it at interest. Incidentally the funding of the debt would provide

THE MASTER BUILDER 57

securities that would serve trade as a species of currency, and would set in motion a long train of benefits that would extend throughout the community. In the funding operation the debts contracted by the States should be included. As to this Hamilton remarked: "The general principle of it seems to be equitable, for it seems difficult to conceive a good reason why the expenses for the particular defense of a part in a common war should not be a common charge, as well as those incurred professedly for the general defense. The defense of each part is that of the whole; and unless the expenditures are brought into a common mass, the tendency must be to add to the calamities suffered by being the most exposed to the ravages of war and increase of burthens."

Hamilton computed the amount of the foreign debt, principal and arrears, at $11,710,378.62; the domestic debt, including that of the States, at $42,414,085.94, — a total of over fifty-four millions with an annual interest charge at existing rates amounting to $4,587,444.81, — a staggering total for a nation whose revenue was then insufficient to meet its current expenses. Nevertheless Hamilton refused to admit that "such a provision would exceed the abilities of the country," but he was "clearly of the opinion that to make it would require the extension of taxation to a degree and to objects which the true interest of the public creditor forbids." He therefore favored a composition, in arranging which there would be strict adherence to the principle "that no change in the rights of creditors ought to be attempted without their voluntary consent; and that this consent ought to be voluntary in fact as well as in name." It followed that "every proposal of a change ought to be in the shape of an appeal to their interests; but not to their necessities." Hamilton then went into details of a funding loan, in which various options were offered to the creditors, including land grants in part payment, and conversion in whole or in part into annuities, several sorts of which were offered. He submitted estimates of how the various plans would work out in practice, and he concluded that the annual revenue which would be required to enable the government to meet its obligations under the scheme and also to maintain its current service would amount to $2,239,163.09, a sum that could be readily provided.

There could not have been a more striking

contrast than there was between the humiliating conditions which actually existed and the grand results which Hamilton designed and confidently expected. The ardent and hopeful tone of his plan, conceived in apparently desperate circumstances, is very marked. He declared: "It cannot but merit particular attention that among ourselves the most enlightened friends of good government are those whose expectations are the highest. To justify and preserve their confidence; to promote the increasing respectability of the American name; to answer the calls of justice; to restore landed property to its due value; to furnish new resources both to agriculture and commerce; to cement more closely the union of the States; to add to their security against foreign attack; to establish public order on the basis of a liberal and upright policy — these are the great and invaluable ends to be secured by a proper and adequate provision at the present period for the support of public credit."

All these great objects were indeed attained, but Hamilton's anticipation of them was at the time regarded as either a pretext made to cajole Congress or else merely an ebullition from his own sanguine nature not to be taken too seriously by sensible people. Senator Maclay of Pennsylvania regarded Hamilton's plans as wildly extravagant in their conception and iniquitous in their practical effect. In his opinion, Hamilton had "a very boyish, giddy manner, and Scotch-Irish people could well call him a 'skite.'" Jackson of Georgia exposed to the House the folly of Hamilton's proposals by pointing out that a funded debt meant national decay. He mentioned England as "a melancholy instance of the ruin attending such engagements." To such a pitch had the "spirit of funding and borrowing been carried in that country" that its national debt was now "a burthen which the most sanguine mind can never contemplate they will ever be relieved from." France also was "considerably enfeebled and languishes under a heavy load of debt." He argued that by funding the debt in America "the same effect must be produced that has taken place in other nations; it must either bring on national bankruptcy, or annihilate her existence as an independent empire."

Such dismal prognostications on the very eve of the Napoleonic era, with its tremendous revelations of national power, were quite common at that time.

THE MASTER BUILDER 61

The long rambling debate that took place in the House when Hamilton's report was taken up for consideration abounds with similar instances of shortsightedness. Many members did not scruple to advise repudiation, in whole or in part. Livermore of New Hampshire admitted that the foreign debt should be provided for, since it was "lent to the United States in real coin, by disinterested persons, not concerned or benefited by the revolution," but that the domestic debt was "for depreciated paper, or services done at exorbitant rates, or for goods or provisions supplied at more than their real worth, by those who received all the benefits arising from our change of condition." True, Congress had pledged its faith to the redemption of issues at their face value, "but this was done on a principle of policy, in order to prevent the rapid depreciation which was taking place." He argued that "money lent in this depreciated and depreciating state can hardly be said to be lent from a spirit of patriotism; it was a mere speculation in public securities."

The distinction between the foreign debt and the domestic was seized by many members as providing a just basis for discrimination. Page of Virginia observed that "our citizens were deeply interested, and, I believe, if they were never to get a farthing for what is owing to them for their services, they would be well paid; they have gained what they aimed at; they have secured their liberties and their laws; they will be satisfied that this House has pledged itself to pay foreigners the generous loans they advanced to us in the day of distress." In the course of the debate the power to do was so often mentioned as implying the right to do that Ames was moved to remark: "I have heard that in the East Indies the stock of the labor and the property of the empire is the property of the Prince; that it is held at his will and pleasure; but this is a slavish doctrine, which I hope we are not prepared to adopt here." As a matter of fact, there had already been extensive scaling of the debt, and the note emissions had been pretty nearly wiped out. To save the public credit from complete collapse, the Continental Congress had entered into definite contracts under the most solemn pledges, and it was upon this select class of securities that it was now proposed to start anew the process of repudiation. But public opinion displayed itself so hostile to such perfidy that the party of repudiation in Congress soon dwindled to insignificance and the struggle finally settled upon two issues, discrimination and assumption.

Weeks of debate ensued, and the deepest impression made by a careful perusal of the record is the inability of members to appreciate the importance of the issues. Much of the tedious and pointless character of their speeches may be ascribed to the lack of the personal presence of the Secretary. There being nothing to focus the debate and exclude the fictitious and irrelevant, it rambled in any direction a speaker's fancy might suggest. Moreover, its quality was impaired because any consideration of motive was of the nature of talking about a man behind his back and this, everyone knows, is very different from saying things to his face. Assertions and innuendos which would hardly have been hazarded had Hamilton been present, or which, had they been made, would have been forthwith met and refuted, were indulged in without restraint. Although one of the reasons given for requiring a written report was that the House would be the better informed, the debate does not indicate that the arguments by which Hamilton had vindicated his proposals had really been apprehended.

The question whether or not any discrimination

could be made between original holders of the public securities and those who had acquired them by purchase was considered at length by Hamilton in his report. The public securities had been at such a heavy discount that now, if they were to be met at face value, speculators would reap large profits. Hamilton put the case of the opposition as strongly as possible. It might be urged that it was unreasonable "to pay twenty shillings in the pound to one who had not given more for it than three or four; and it is added that it would be hard to aggravate the misfortune of the first owner, who, probably through necessity, parted with his property at so great a loss, by obliging him to contribute to the profit of the person who had speculated on his distresses." Nevertheless, Hamilton submitted considerations showing that discrimination would be "equally unjust and impolitic, as highly injurious even to the original holders of public securities, as ruinous to public credit." It is unnecessary to repeat the lucid argument by which Hamilton demonstrated the soundness of his position, for security of transfer is now well understood to be an essential element of public credit; but the special point of interest is that the debate simply ignored Hamilton's

THE MASTER BUILDER

argument and rambled along over the superficial aspects of the case, dwelling upon the sorrows of those who had parted with their holdings, and exhibiting their situation as the most important matter to be considered.

Madison was most active in making that branch of the case the leading issue, and in a series of elaborate speeches which cannot now be read without regret, he urged that the present holders should be allowed only the highest market price previously recorded, and that the residue should go to the original holders. Boudinot at once pointed out that there was nothing on record to show who might be an original bona fide holder. Great quantities of the certificates of indebtedness had, as a mere matter of convenience, been issued to government clerks who afterwards distributed them among those who furnished supplies to the government or who performed services entitling them to pay. He mentioned that he himself appeared on the record as original holder in cases wherein he had really acted in behalf of his neighbors to relieve them of the trouble of personal appearance. Madison's proposition would therefore invest him with a legal title to property which really belonged to others. But this and other evidence of the real effect of Madison's proposal failed to move him, further than to cause him to declare that "all that he wished was that the claims of the original holders, not less than those of the actual holders, should be fairly examined and justly decided." Finally Benson of New York gave him a shrewd home thrust that plainly embarrassed him. He put the question whether, if he had purchased a certificate from Madison, and the Treasury withheld part of the amount for Madison as the original holder, Madison would keep the money? "I ask," said Benson, "whether he would take advantage of the law against me, and refuse to give me authority to take it up in his name?" Madison evaded the query by saying that everything would depend upon the circumstances of any particular case, and that circumstances were conceivable in which the most tender conscience need not refrain from taking the benefit of what the government had determined.

The debate on Madison's discrimination amendment lasted from the eleventh to the twenty-second day of February — Washington's birthday. The House did honor to the day when it rejected Madison's motion by the crushing vote of 36 to 13. With that, his pretensions to the leadership of the House quite disappeared.

The assumption of state debts was the subject of a debate in committee of the whole which lasted from the twenty-third of February to the second of March. New factional lines now revealed a supposed diversity of interest of the several States. The false notions of finance then current were illustrated by an argument that was in continual use, either on the floor or in the lobby. Members would figure how much their States would have to pay as their share of the debt that would be assumed, and on that basis would reach conclusions as to how their States stood to win or lose by the transaction. By this reckoning, of course, the great gainer would appear to be the State upon whom the chances of war had piled the largest debt. This calculation made Burke of South Carolina, usually an opponent of anything coming from Hamilton, a strong advocate of assumption. He told the House that "if the present question was lost, he was almost certain it would end in her bankruptcy, for she [South Carolina] was no more able to grapple with her enormous debt than a boy of twelve years of age is able to grapple with a giant." Livermore, representing a State never within the actual field of military operations, at once replied: "I conceive that the debt of South Carolina, or Massachusetts, or of an individual, has nothing to do with our deliberations. If they have involved themselves in debt, it is their misfortune, and they must extricate themselves as well as they can." On a later occasion Stone of Maryland, another State that lay outside the track of war, gave the leading war-debt States an admonition of the kind that adds insult to injury, saying "however inconvenient it may be to Massachusetts or South Carolina to make a bold exertion, and nobly bear the burthens of their present debt, I believe in the end it would be found to conduce greatly to their advantage." Burke made a crushing rejoinder. "Was Maryland like South Carolina constantly grappling with the enemy during the whole war? There is not a road in the State but has witnessed the ravages of war; plantations were destroyed, and the skeletons of houses, to this day, point out to the traveler the route of the British army; her citizens were exposed to every violence, their capital taken, and their country almost overrun by the enemy; men, women, and children murdered by the Indians and Tories; all the personal property consumed, and now is it to be wondered at that she is not able to make exertions equal with other States, who have been generally in an undisturbed condition?"

The argument pressed by the advocates of assumption was that the state debts contracted during the Revolutionary War were for the common defense, and that, unless these were assumed by the general government, the adoption of the new Constitution would do injury by withdrawing revenue resources which the States had formerly possessed. This position at the present day seems reasonable enough, but it is certain that at that time people worked themselves into a genuine rage over the matter and were able to persuade themselves into a sincere belief that it was outrageous the unfortunate States should expect the others to bear their troubles, and that Hamilton was a great rogue for proposing such a scheme. Writing in his private diary, Maclay characterized the plan as "a monument of political absurdity," and he was in the habit of referring to Hamilton's supporters as his "gladiators" and as a "corrupt squadron."

On the whole the records make painful reading. The prevailing tone of public life was one of dull and narrow provincialism, at times thickening into stupidity, at times sharpening into spite, although ordinarily made respectable by a serious attitude to life and by a stolid fortitude in facing whatever the distracted times might present. It was the influence of a few great men that made America a nation. If one is not subject to the spirit of ancestor worship that has long ruled American history, one is bound to say that — apart from some forceful pamphleteering of transient purpose—the voluminous political literature of the formative period displays much pedantic erudition but has little that goes really deep. The *Federalist*, the artillery of a hard fought battle, is a striking exception. So, too, is the series of reports by Hamilton. But his plans could not prevail by force of reason against the general spirit of selfish particularism. Although on March 2 a motion adverse to assumption in committee of the whole was defeated by a vote of 28 to 22, it was then known that a majority could not be procured for enactment, and on April 12 the assumption bill was defeated outright in the House, 31 to 29. Maclay, who went over to the House from the Senate to witness the event, gloated over the defeat in his diary:

"Sedgwick, from Boston, pronounced a funeral

oration over it. He was called to order; some confusion ensued; he took his hat and went out. When he returned, his visage bore the visible marks of weeping. Fitzsimmons reddened like scarlet; his eyes were brimful. Clymer's color, always pale, now merged to a deadly white; his lips quivered, and his nether jaw shook with convulsive motions; his head, neck, and breast contracted with gesticulations resembling those of a turkey or goose nearly strangled in the act of deglutition. Benson bungled like a shoemaker who has lost his end. . . . Wadsworth hid his grief under the rim of a round hat. Boudinot's wrinkles rose in ridges and the angles of his mouth were depressed and assumed a curve resembling a horse's shoe."

The defeat did not discourage Hamilton. He had successfully handled a more difficult situation in getting New York to ratify the Constitution, and, resorting now to the same means he had then employed, he used pressure of interest to move those who could not be stirred by reason. The intense concern felt by members in the choice of the site of the national capital supplied him with the leverage which he brought to bear on the situation. Most of the members were more stirred by that question than by any other before

72 WASHINGTON AND HIS COLLEAGUES

Congress. It was a prominent topic in Madison's correspondence from the time the Constitution was adopted. Maclay's diary abounds with references to the subject. Some of his bitterest sentences are penned about the conduct of those who preferred some other site to that on the Susquehanna River which he knew to be the best because he lived there himself. Bargaining among the members as to the selection had been going on almost from the first. As early as April 26, 1789, before Washington had been installed in his office, Maclay mentions a meeting "to concert some measures for the removal of Congress." Thereafter notices of pending deals appear frequently in his diary. After the defeat of the assumption bill, the diary notes the activity of Hamilton in this matter. An entry of June 14, 1790, ascribes to Robert Morris the statement that "Hamilton said he wanted one vote in the Senate and five in the House of Representatives; that he was willing and would agree to place the permanent residence of Congress at Germantown or Falls of the Delaware (Trenton), if he would procure him those votes." Although definite knowledge is unattainable, one gets the impression, in following the devious course of these intrigues, that had

THE MASTER BUILDER 73

Pennsylvania interests been united they could have decided the site of the national capital; but the delegation was divided over the relative merits of the Delaware and the Susquehanna as well as on the question of assumption. Hamilton's efforts in this quarter were ineffectual, and the winning combination was finally arranged elsewhere and otherwise by the aid of Jefferson.

Thomas Jefferson was at this time forty-seven years old, and owing both to seniority and to the distinguished positions he had held, he ranked as the most illustrious member of the Administration. His correspondence at this period shows that he was fully aware of the importance of the crisis, and he did not overrate it when he wrote to James Monroe, June 20, 1790, that, unless the measures of the Administration were successful, "our credit will burst and vanish, and the States separate to take care everyone of itself." In this letter Jefferson outlined the compromise that was actually adopted by Congress. The strongest opposition to the assumption bill had come from Virginia, although Maryland, Georgia, and New Hampshire also opposed it, and the Middle States were divided. Jefferson was able to get enough Southern votes to carry assumption in return for enough votes from Hamilton's adherents to carry the Potomac site. An agreement was reached at a dinner given by Jefferson to which he invited Hamilton and Madison. According to this arrangement, the capital was to remain in Philadelphia for ten years and after that to be on the Potomac River in a district ten miles square to be selected by the President. The residence act was approved July 16, 1790; the funding and assumption measures, now combined in one bill, became law on August 4.

After Jefferson turned against the Administration, his participation in the passage of the assumption bill was such an awkward circumstance that he discredited his own intelligence by professing that he "was most ignorantly and innocently made to hold the candle" to Hamilton's "game." In reality the public service Jefferson then performed was the most useful in all his long and fruitful career. But for this action, the Declaration of Independence, to the drafting of which he owes his greatest fame, might now be figuring among the historical documents of lost causes, like similar elaborate statements of principle made during the Commonwealth period in England. Had the national forces failed at the critical period of financial organization, and the States, bankrupt by the revolutionary struggle, been left in the lurch, the republic would have followed the usual course of disintegration displayed by federations from the time of the Greek amphictyonies down to that of the Holy Roman Empire.

The charge was made soon after Hamilton's victory that it was largely due to the influence of speculators. The advance in the market value of securities produced by Hamilton's measures certainly gave an opportunity to speculators of which they availed themselves with the unscrupulous activity characteristic of the sordid tribe. Jefferson has left an account of "the base scramble." "Couriers and relay horses by land, and swift sailing pilot boats by sea, were flying in all directions. Active partners and agents were associated and employed in every state, town, and country neighborhood, and this paper was bought up at five shillings, and even as low as two shillings in the pound, before the holder knew that Congress had already provided for its assumption at par. Immense sums were thus filched from the poor and ignorant, and fortunes accumulated by those who had themselves been poor enough before."

This account is highly colored. The struggle

76 WASHINGTON AND HIS COLLEAGUES

was too close, and the issue was long too doubtful, to admit of speculative preparations extending to every "town and country neighborhood." If speculation took place on such a large scale, it must have been also taking risks on a large scale, for assumption was not assured until Jefferson himself put his shoulder to the wheel. The lack of means for prompt diffusion of intelligence naturally provided large opportunity for speculation by those in a position to keep well-informed, and undoubtedly large profits were made; but the circumstances were such that it seems most probable that profits were less than market opportunities would have allowed had not the issue been so long in doubt. Nevertheless there was much speculative activity, and the charge was soon made that it extended into Congress.[1]

[1] This charge was put forth by John Taylor in pamphlets printed in 1793 and 1794, in which he reviewed the financial policy of the Administration and gave a list of Congressmen who had invested in the public funds. The facts on which this charge rests have been collected and examined by Professor Beard in his *Economic Origins of Jeffersonian Democracy*. His analysis shows that out of sixty-four members of the House, twenty-nine were security holders, and of these twenty-one voted for and eight voted against assumption. But the facts disclosed do not sustain his theory that the issue was essentially a conflict between capitalism and agrarianism. The assumption bill was lifted to its place on the statute book through the leverage exerted by Hamilton and Jefferson, with Washington's prestige as their fulcrum. The characters of these three men resist schemes of classification

THE MASTER BUILDER

The passage of assumption was the turning point. Other important measures followed, but none of them met with difficulties which the Administration could not overcome by ordinary methods of persuasion and appeal. A national bank was authorized by an act approved on February 25, 1791. Hamilton's famous report on manufactures, a masterly analysis of the sources of national wealth and of the means of improving them, was sent to Congress on December 5, 1791. Upon his recommendation Congress established the mint, the only point which excited controversy being Hamilton's proposal that the coins should be stamped with the head of the President in whose administration they were issued. This suggestion was rejected on the ground that it smacked too much of the practice of monarchies. The queer totemistic designs of American coinage are a consequence of this decision.

The formation of national government by voluntary agreement is a unique event. The

---

according to economic interest. The principal value of analysis of the economic elements of the struggle is to protect from undervaluation the motives that actuated the opposition to Hamilton's measures. The historian has the advantage of a perspective denied to participants in events, and this fact is apt to turn unduly to the discredit of lost causes.

explanation of this peculiar result in the case of America is the unifying influence of Hamilton's measures. They interested in the support of the government economic forces strong enough to counteract the separatist tendencies that had always before broken up states unless they were held together by sheer might of power in their rulers. The means employed have been cited as evidence in support of the economic interpretation of history now in fashion. Government, it is true, like every other form of life, must meet the fundamental needs of subsistence and defense, but this truism supplies no explanation of the particular mode of doing so that may be adopted. Those needs account for motion but not for direction. Human will, discernment, and purpose enter and complicate the situation in a way that makes theories of determinism appear absurd. No one has ever contended that Hamilton was prompted by an economic motive in giving up his law practice to accept public office. He did so against the remonstrances of his friends, whose predictions that what he would get out of it for himself would be calumny, persecution, and loss of fortune, were all fully verified; but he possessed a nature which found its happiness in bringing high ideals to grand fulfillment, and in applying his powers to that object he let everything else go. Hamilton's career is one of the greatest of those facts that baffle attempts to reduce history to an exhibition of the play of economic forces.

CHAPTER IV

ALARUMS AND EXCURSIONS

THE Shakespearian stage direction which heads this chapter appropriately describes the course of administrative experience while Washington was trying to get from Congress the means of sustaining the responsibilities with which he was charged by his office. Events did not stand still because for a time anything like national government had ceased. Before Washington left Mount Vernon he had been disquieted by reports of Indian troubles in the West, and of intrigues by Great Britain — which still retained posts that according to the treaty of peace belonged to the United States, — and by Spain which held the lower Mississippi. Washington applied himself to these matters as soon as he was well in office, but he was much hindered in his arrangements by apathy or indifference in Congress. He noted in his diary for May 1, 1790, communications made to him of a disposition among members of Congress "to pay little attention to the Western country because they were of the opinion it would soon shake off its dependence on this, and in the meantime would be burdensome to it." From a letter of Gen. Rufus Putnam, one of the organizers of the Ohio company, it appears that in July, 1789, Ames of Massachusetts put these queries to him: "Can we retain the western country with the government of the United States? And if we can, what use will it be to them?" Putnam wrote a labored article to the effect that it was both feasible and desirable to hold the West, but the character of his arguments shows that there was then a poor prospect of success. At that time no one could have anticipated the Napoleonic wars which ended all European competition for the possession of the Mississippi valley, and, as it were, tossed that region into the hands of the United States. There was strong opposition in Congress to pursuing any course that would require maintenance of an army or navy. Some held that it was a great mistake to have a war department, and that there would be time enough to create one in case war should actually arrive.

In a message to the Senate, August 7, 1789,

Washington had urged the importance of "some uniform and effective system for the militia of the United States," saying that he was "particularly anxious" it should receive early attention. On January 18, 1790, General Knox submitted to Congress a plan to which there are frequent references in Washington's diary, showing the special interest he took in the subject. The report laid down principles which have long since been embraced by European nations, but which have just recently been recognized by the United States. It asserts: "That it is the indispensable duty of every nation to establish all necessary institutions for its protection and defense; that it is a capital security to a free state for the great body of the people to possess a competent knowledge of the military art; that every man of the proper age and ability of body is firmly bound by the social compact to perform, personally, his proportion of military duty for the defense of the State; that all men of the legal military age should be armed, enrolled, and held responsible for different degrees of military service." In furtherance of these principles a scheme was submitted providing for military service by the citizens of the United States beginning at eighteen years of age and terminating at sixty.

The response of Congress was the Act of April 30, 1790, authorizing a military establishment "to the number of one thousand two hundred and sixteen non-commissioned officers, privates, and musicians," with permission to the President to call State Militia into service if need be, "in protecting the inhabitants of the frontiers." Washington, in noting in his diary his approval of the act, observed that it was not "adequate to the exigencies of the government and the protection it is intended to afford."

The Indian troubles in the Southwest were made particularly serious by the ability of the head-chief of the Creek nation, Alexander McGillivray, the authentic facts of whose career might seem too wildly improbable even for the uses of melodrama. His grandmother was a full-blooded Creek of high standing in the nation. She had a daughter by Captain Marchand, a French officer. This daughter, who is described as a bewitching beauty, was taken to wife by Lachland McGillivray, a Scotchman engaged in the Indian trade. A son was born who, at the age of ten, was sent by his father to Charleston to be educated, where he remained nearly seven years receiving instruction both in English and Latin. This son, Alexander, was intended by his father for civilized life, and when he was seventeen he was placed with a business house in Savannah. During the Revolutionary War the father took the Tory side and his property was confiscated. The son took refuge with his Indian kinsfolk, and acquired in their councils an ascendancy which also extended to the Seminole tribe. His position and influence made his favor an important object with all powers having American interests. During the war the British conferred upon him the rank and pay of a colonel. In 1784, as the representative of the Creek and Seminole nations, he formed a treaty of alliance with Spain, by the terms of which he became a Spanish commissary with the rank and pay of a colonel.

Against the State of Georgia, the Creek nation had grievances which McGillivray was able to voice with a vigor and an eloquence that compelled attention. It was the old story, so often repeated in American history, of encroachments upon Indian territory. Attempts at negotiation had been made by the old government, and these were now renewed by Washington with no better result. McGillivray met the commissioners, but left on finding that they had no intention of restoring the

ALARUMS AND EXCURSIONS

Indian lands that had been taken. A formidable Indian war seemed imminent, but Washington, whose own frontier experience made him well versed in Indian affairs, judged correctly that the way to handle the situation was to induce McGillivray to come to New York, though, as he noted in his diary, the matter must be so managed that the "government might not appear to be an agent in it, or suffer in its dignity if the attempt to get him here should not succeed." With his habitual caution, Washington considered the point whether he could send out an agent without consulting the Senate on the appointment, and he instructed General Knox "to take the opinion of the Chief Justice of the United States and the Secretary of the Treasury." The assurances obtained were such that Washington selected an experienced frontier commander, Colonel Marinus Willett of New York, and impressed upon him the importance of bringing the Indian chiefs to New York, pointing out "the arguments justifiable for him to use to effect this, with such lures as respected McGillivray personally, and might be held out to them."

Colonel Willett was altogether successful, though the inducements he offered were probably aided by McGillivray's desire to visit New York and meet General Washington. Other chiefs accompanied him, and on their way they received many official attentions. An incident which occurred at Guilford Court House, South Carolina, displays McGillivray's character in a kindly light. A woman whose husband had been killed by Creek Indians and who with her children had been made captive, visited McGillivray to thank him for effecting their release, and it was disclosed that he had since that time been contributing to the support of the family. At New York, the recently organized Tammany Society turned out in costumes supposed to represent Indian attire and escorted the visiting chiefs to Federal Hall. Eventually Washington himself went to Federal Hall in his coach of state and in all the trappings of official dignity, to sign the treaty concluded with the Indians. The treaty, which laid down the pattern subsequently followed by the government in its dealings with the Indians, recognized the claims of the Creek nation to part of the territory it claimed, and gave compensation for the part it relinquished by an annuity of fifteen hundred dollars for the tribe, and an annuity of one hundred dollars for each of the principal chiefs.

ALARUMS AND EXCURSIONS

For his part in the transaction McGillivray was commissioned an agent of the United States with the rank of brigadier-general, a position which he sustained with dignity. He was six feet tall, spare in frame, erect in carriage. His eyes were large, dark, and piercing; his forehead, wider at the top than just above the eyes, was so high and broad as to be almost bulging. When he was a British colonel, he wore the uniform of that rank; when in the Spanish service, he wore the military dress of that country; and after Washington appointed him a brigadier-general he sometimes wore the uniform of the American army, but never in the presence of Spaniards. In different parts of his dominions he had good houses where he practised generous hospitality. His influence was shaken by his various political alliances, and before he died in 1793 he had lost much of his authority.

In the course of these negotiations Washington had an experience with the Senate which thereafter affected his official behavior. The debates of the constitutional convention indicated an expectation that the Senate would act as a privy council to the President; and Washington — intent above all things on doing his duty — tried to treat it as such. In company with General

88 WASHINGTON AND HIS COLLEAGUES

Knox he went to the Senate chamber, prepared to explain his negotiations with the Indian chiefs, but he forthwith experienced the truth of the proverb that although you may lead a horse to water you cannot make him drink. In his diary for August 22, 1789, Maclay gave a characteristic account of the scene. Washington presided, taking the Vice-President's chair. "He rose and told us bluntly that he had called on us for our advice and consent to some propositions respecting the treaty to be held with the Southern Indians. Said he had brought General Knox with him who was well acquainted with the business." A statement was read giving a schedule of the propositions on which the advice of the Senate was asked. Maclay relates that he called for the reading of the treaties and other documents referred to in the statement. "I cast an eye at the President of the United States. I saw he wore an aspect of stern displeasure." There was a manifest reluctance of the Senate to proceed with the matter in the President's presence, and finally a motion was made to refer the business to a committee of five. A sharp debate followed in which "the President of the United States started up in a violent fret. 'This defeats every purpose of my

ALARUMS AND EXCURSIONS

coming here' were the first words that he said. He then went on to say that he had brought his Secretary of War with him to give any necessary information; that the Secretary knew all about the business, and yet he was delayed and could not go on with the matter." The situation evidently became strained. Maclay relates: "A pause for some time ensued. We waited for him to withdraw. He did so with a discontented air."

The privy council function of the Senate was thus in effect abolished by its own action. Thereafter the President had practically no choice save to conclude matters subject to subsequent ratification by the Senate. It soon became the practice of the Senate to restrict the President's power of appointment by conditioning it upon the approval of the Senators from the State in which an appointment was made. The clause providing for the advice and consent of the Senate was among the changes made in the original draft to conciliate the small States, but it was not supposed that the practical effect would be to allow Senators to dictate appointments. It was observed in the *Federalist* that "there will be no exertion of choice on the part of Senators." Nevertheless there was some uneasiness on the point. In a letter of May

31, 1789, Ames remarked that "the meddling of the Senate in appointments is one of the least defensible parts of the Constitution," and with prophetic insight he foretold that "the number of the Senators, the secrecy of their doings, would shelter them, and a corrupt connection between those who appoint to office and the officers themselves would be created."

Washington had to submit to senatorial dictation almost at the outset of his administration, the Senate refusing to confirm his nomination of Benjamin Fishbourn for the place of naval officer at Savannah. The only details to be had about this affair are those given in a special message of August 6, 1789, from which it appears that Washington was not notified of the grounds of the Senate's objection. He defended his selection on the ground that Fishbourn had a meritorious record as an army officer, had held distinguished positions in the state government of Georgia which testified public confidence, and moreover was actually holding, by virtue of state appointment, an office similar to that to which Washington desired to appoint him. The appointment was, in fact, no more than the transfer to the federal service of an official of approved administrative

ALARUMS AND EXCURSIONS 91

experience, and was of such manifest propriety that it seems most likely that the rejection was due to local political intrigue using the Georgia Senators as its tool. The office went to Lachlan McIntosh, who was a prominent Georgia politician. Over ten years before he had killed in a duel Button Gwinnett, a signer of the Declaration of Independence. Gwinnett was the challenger and McIntosh was badly wounded in the duel, but the affair caused a feud that long disturbed Georgia politics, and through the agency of the Senate it was able to reach and annoy the President of the United States.

At the time when Washington was inaugurated both North Carolina and Rhode Island were outside the Union. The national government was a new and doubtful enterprise, remote from and unfamiliar to the mass of the people. To turn their thoughts toward the new Administration it seemed to be good policy for Washington to make tours. The notes made by Washington in his diary indicate that the project was his own notion, but both Hamilton and Knox cordially approved it and Madison "saw no impropriety" in it. Therefore, shortly after the recess of the first session of Congress, Washington started on a trip through the Northern States, pointedly avoiding Rhode Island, then a foreign country. It was during this tour that a question of etiquette occurred about which there was a great stir at the time. John Hancock, then Governor of Massachusetts, did not call upon Washington but wrote inviting Washington to stay at his house, and when this invitation was declined, he wrote again inviting the President to dinner *en famille*. Washington again declined, and this time the failure of the Governor to pay his respects to the President of the United States was the talk of the town. Some of Hancock's aides now called with excuses on the score of his illness. Washington noted in his diary, "I informed them in explicit terms that I should not see the Governor unless it was at my own lodgings." This incident occurred on Saturday evening, and the effect was such that Governor Hancock called in person on Sunday. The affair was the subject of much comment not to Governor Hancock's advantage. Washington's church-going habits on this trip afford no small evidence of the patient consideration which he paid to every point of duty. In New York, he attended Episcopal church service regularly once every Sunday. On his northern tour he went

ALARUMS AND EXCURSIONS 93

to the Episcopal church in the morning, and then showed his respect for the dominant religious system of New England by attending the Congregational church in the afternoon. His northern tour lasted from October 15 to November 13, 1789, and was attended by popular manifestations that must have promoted the spread of national sentiment. On November 21, 1789, North Carolina came into the Union, and Rhode Island followed on May 29, 1790. Washington started on a tour of the Southern States on March 21, 1791, in which he covered more than seventeen hundred miles in sixty-six days, and was received with grand demonstrations at all the towns he visited.

While he was making these tours, which in the days before the railroad and the telegraph were practically the only efficacious means of establishing the new government in the thoughts and feelings of the people, he was much concerned about frontier troubles, and with good reason, as he well knew the deficiency of the means that Congress had allowed. The tiny army of the United States was under the command of Lieutenant-Colonel Josiah Harmar, with the brevet rank of general. In October, 1790, Harmar led his troops, nearly four-fifths of which were new levies of militia, against the Indians who had been disturbing the western frontier. The expedition was a succession of blunders and failures which were due more to the rude and undisciplined character of the material that Harmar had to work with than to his personal incapacity. Harmar did succeed in destroying five Indian villages with their stores of corn, but their inhabitants had warning enough to escape and were able to take prompt vengeance. A detachment of troops was ambushed and badly cut up. The design had been to push on to the upper course of the Wabash, but so many horses had been stolen by the Indians that the expedition was crippled. As a result, Harmar marched his troops back again, professing to believe that punishment had been inflicted upon the Indians that would be a severe lesson to them. What really happened was that the Indians were encouraged to think that they were more than a match for any army which the settlers could send against them, and before long news came of the destruction of settlements and the massacre of their inhabitants. "Unless," wrote Rufus Putnam to Washington, "Government speedily sends a body of troops for our protection, we are a ruined people."

ALARUMS AND EXCURSIONS

Washington did what he could. He sent to Congress Putnam's letter and other frontier communications, but Congress, which was stubbornly opposed to creating a national army, replied, when the need was demonstrated, that the militia of the several States were available. The Government was without means of protecting the Indians against abuse and injustice or of protecting the settlers against the savage retaliations that naturally followed. The dilemma was stated with sharp distinctness in correspondence which passed between Washington and Hamilton in April, 1791. Washington wrote that it was a hopeless undertaking to keep peace on the frontier "whilst land-jobbing and the disorderly conduct of our borderers are suffered with impunity; and while the States individually are omitting no occasion to intermeddle in matters which belong to the general Government." Hamilton in reply went to the root of the matter. "Our system is such as still to leave the public peace of the Union at the mercy of each state government." He proceeded to give a concrete instance: "For example, a party comes from a county of Virginia into Pennsylvania, and wantonly murders some friendly Indians. The national Government, instead of having power to apprehend the murderers and bring them to justice, is obliged to make a representation to that of Pennsylvania; that of Pennsylvania, again, is to make a requisition of that of Virginia. And whether the murderers shall be brought to justice at all must depend upon the particular policy, and energy, and good disposition of two state governments, and the efficacy of the provisions of their respective laws. And security of other States and the money of all are at the discretion of one. These things require a remedy; but when that will come, God knows."

Toward the close of its last session, the First Congress was induced to pass an act "for raising and adding another regiment to the military establishment of the United States and for making further provision for the protection of the frontiers." The further provision authorized the President to employ "troops enlisted under the denomination of levies" for a term not exceeding six months and in number not exceeding two thousand. The law thus made it compulsory that the troops should move while still raw and untrained. Congress had fixed the pay of the privates at three dollars a month, from which ninety cents were deducted, and it had been

ALARUMS AND EXCURSIONS

necessary to scrape the streets and even the prisons of the seaboard cities for men willing to enlist upon such terms. Washington gave the command to General Arthur St. Clair, whose military experience should have made him a capable commander, but he was then in bad health and unable to handle the situation under the conditions imposed upon him. General Harmar, enlightened by his own experience, predicted that such an army would certainly be defeated.

The campaign was intended as an expedition to chastise the Indians so that they would be deterred from molesting the settlers, but it resulted in a disaster that greatly encouraged Indian depredations. As the army approached the Indian towns, a body of the militia deserted, and it was reported to St. Clair that they intended to plunder the supplies. He sent one of his regular regiments after them, thus reducing his available force to about fourteen hundred men. On November 3, 1791, this force camped on the eastern fork of Wabash. Before daybreak the next morning the Indians made a sudden attack, taking the troops by surprise and throwing them into disorder. It was the story of Braddock's defeat over again. The troops were surrounded by foes that they could not see and could not reach. Indian marksmen picked off the gunners until the artillery was silenced; then the Indians rushed in and seized the guns. In the combat there were both conspicuous exploits of valor and disgraceful scenes of cowardice. In that dark hour St. Clair showed undaunted courage. He was in the front of the fight, and several times he headed charges. He seemed to have a charmed life, for although eight bullets pierced his clothes, one cutting away a lock of the thick gray hair that flowed from under his three-cornered hat, he escaped without a wound. Finally defeat became a rout which St. Clair was powerless to check. Pushed aside in the rush of fugitives, he was left in a position of great peril. If the Indian pursuit had been persistent, few might have escaped, but the Indians stopped to plunder the camp. Nevertheless six hundred and thirty men were killed and over two hundred and eighty wounded, with small loss to the Indians.

Washington's reception of the news illustrates both his iron composure and the gusts of passion under which it sometimes gave way. The details are unquestionably authentic, as they were communicated by Washington's secretary who witnessed the scene. Washington was having a dinner party when an officer arrived at the door and sent word that he was the bearer of dispatches from the Western army. The secretary went out to him, but the officer said his instructions were to deliver the dispatches to the President in person. Washington then went to the officer and received the terrible news. He returned to the table as though nothing had happened, and everything went on as usual. After dinner there was a reception in Mrs. Washington's drawing-room and the President, as was his custom, spoke courteously to every lady in the room. By ten o'clock all the visitors had gone and Washington began to pace the floor at first without any change of manner, but soon he began to show emotional excitement and he broke out suddenly: "It's all over! St. Clair is defeated — routed, — the officers nearly all killed — the men by wholesale, — the rout complete, — too shocking to think of,— and a surprise into the bargain!"

When near the door in his agitated march about the room, he stopped and burst forth, "Yes, here on this very spot I took leave of him; I wished him success and honor; 'You have your instructions,' I said, 'from the Secretary of War; I had a strict eye to them, and will add one word — Beware of a surprise! You know how the Indians fight us!' He went off with that as my last solemn warning thrown into his ears. And yet, to suffer that army to be cut to pieces — hacked, butchered, tomahawked — by a surprise! O God, O God, he's worse than a murderer! How can he answer it to his country! The blood of the slain is upon him — the curse of the widows and orphans — the curse of Heaven!"

The secretary relates that this torrent of passion burst forth in appalling tones. The President's frame shook. "More than once he threw his hands up as he hurled imprecations upon St. Clair." But at length he got his feelings under control, and after a pause he remarked, "I will hear him without prejudice. He shall have full justice." St. Clair was, indeed, treated with marked leniency. A committee of the House reported that the failure of the expedition could not "be imputed to his conduct, either at any time before or during the action." St. Clair was continued in his position as Governor of the Northwest Territory and remained there until 1802.

Notwithstanding the dire results of relying on casual levies, Congress was still stubbornly opposed

ALARUMS AND EXCURSIONS

to creating an effective force under national control, and in this attitude to some extent reflected even frontier sentiment. Ames in a letter of January 13, 1792, wrote that "even the views of the western people, whose defense has been undertaken by government, have been unfriendly to the Secretary of War and to the popularity of the Government. They wish to be hired as volunteers, at two-thirds of a dollar a day to fight the Indians. They are averse to the regulars." By the Act of March 5, 1792, Congress authorized three additional regiments, with the proviso, however, that they "shall be discharged as soon as the United States shall be at peace with the Indian tribes." This legislation, nevertheless, was a great practical improvement on the previous act. General Wayne, who now took command, was fortunately circumstanced in that he was under no pressure to move against the Indians. Public opinion favored a return to negotiation, so that he had time to get his troops under good discipline. He did not move the main body of his troops until the summer of 1794, and on August 20, he inflicted a smashing defeat on the Indians, at a place known as the Fallen Timbers, followed up the victory by punitive expeditions to the

Indian towns, and burned their houses and crops. The campaign was a complete success. The Indians were so humbled by their losses that they sued for peace, and negotiations began which were concluded in the summer of 1795 by the treaty of Greenville, under which the Northwestern tribes ceded an extensive territory to the United States.

It was notorious that the trouble which the American authorities had experienced with the Indians had been largely due to the activity of British agents. In his report Wayne noted that the destruction effected by his troops included "the houses, stores, and property of Colonel Mc-Kee, the British agent, and principal stimulator of the war now existing between the United States and the savages." A sharp correspondence took place between Wayne and Major William Campbell, commanding a British post on the Miami. Campbell protested against the approach of Wayne's army, "no war existing between Great Britain and America." Wayne assented to this statement, and then asked what he meant "by taking post far within the well known and acknowledged limits of the United States." Campbell rejoined that he had acted under orders and as to his right, that was a matter which were best left to "the ambassadors of our different nations." Campbell refused to obey Wayne's demand to withdraw, and Wayne ignored Campbell's threat to fire if he were approached too close. Wayne reported that the only notice he took of this threat was "by immediately setting fire to and destroying everything within view of the fort, and even under the muzzles of the guns." "Had Mr. Campbell carried his threats into execution," added Wayne, "it is more than probable he would have experienced a storm." No collision actually took place at that time but there was created a situation which, unless it were removed by diplomacy, must have eventually brought on war.

CHAPTER V

TRIBUTE TO THE ALGERINES

At the time when Washington took office, the captains and crews of two American vessels, which had been seized by Algerine Corsairs in 1785, still remained in captivity. The Continental Congress had made some efforts in their behalf which were contemptuously received. The Dey of Algiers did not wish any treaty with the United States; but he did want $59,496.00 for the twenty-one captives whom he then held. Farther than that negotiation had not progressed. Agents of the United States were advised that, if such a high amount were paid, the Corsairs would pursue American vessels in preference to those of any other nation, and that the shrewd thing would be to pretend indifference to the fate of the captives. This advice was acted upon even to the extent of cutting off the supplies which had been forwarded to the captives through the Spanish consul at

TRIBUTE TO THE ALGERINES 105

Algiers. The summary method which was pursued was that of dishonoring bills drawn by him to cover his expenditures.

Jefferson, who while Minister to France had been closely connected with these proceedings, was called upon by Congress for a report upon them, not long after he took office as Secretary of State. This report, December 28, 1790, set forth the fact that the Mediterranean trade, which had employed from eighty to one hundred ships with about twelve hundred seamen, had been almost destroyed. In the interest of the negotiations, it had been necessary "to suffer the captives and their friends to believe for a while, that no attention was paid to them, no notice taken of their letters," and they were "still under this impression." Jefferson contented himself with submitting the facts in the case, remarking that "upon the whole it rests with Congress to decide between war, tribute, and ransom. If war, they will consider how far our own resources shall be called forth, and how far they will enable the Executive to engage, in the forms of the Constitution, the coöperation of other Powers. If tribute or ransom, it will rest with them to limit and provide the amount; and with the

Executive, observing the same constitutional forms, to make arrangements for employing it to the best advantage."

The problem which Jefferson thus put before Congress was a singularly difficult one. Among the captives was Captain Richard O'Brien, whose ship, the *Dauphin* of Philadelphia, was taken July 30, 1785. He had a ready pen and, apparently, had unrestricted access to the mails. His letters were those of a shrewd observer and depicted a situation that bristled with perplexity. The Algerines had about a dozen vessels, their armament ranging from ten to thirty-six guns, but of these vessels only two belonged to the Government, the others being private ventures. Though they preyed on merchantmen, they avoided engagements, and did not come out at all if there were vessels cruising for them. A blockade was effective only while it lasted. Whenever it was raised, out came the Corsairs again. An occasional bombardment of their port did not cow them and had no permanent effect. A French official described it as being "like breaking glass windows with guineas." The Algerines made treaties with some Powers in consideration of tribute but refused peace to others on any terms, as they did not desire to shut out all opportunity for their time-honored sport of piracy.

Congress was slow to take action of any kind. In January, 1791, Maclay noted that a committee had decided that the Mediterranean trade could not be preserved without an armed force to protect it, and that a navy should be established as soon as the Treasury was in a position to bear the expense. Meanwhile the President began fresh negotiations, which were attended by singular fatality. Thomas Barclay, who had some diplomatic experience, was commissioned to go to the Emperor of Morocco. When Barclay reached Gibraltar, he was taken ill, and, after being removed to Lisbon, he died. Admiral John Paul Jones was then appointed special commissioner to arrange for the ransom of the captives. As he had then left the Russian service and was living in Paris, it was supposed that his services would be available, but he died before the commission could reach him. The delay caused by these events was made so much worse by the slow transmission of intelligence that two years elapsed before a fresh start was made by placing the conduct of matters in the hands of Colonel David Humphreys, then Minister to Portugal. Humphreys had gone as far as Gibraltar on his mission when he learned that a truce had been suddenly arranged between Portugal and Algiers. This was alarming news, since it meant that the Algerines could now pass into the Atlantic from which they had been excluded by Portuguese war-vessels stationed in the strait of Gibraltar. "I have not slept since the receipt of the news of this the hellish plot," wrote Edward Church, the United States consul at Lisbon. Church was energetic in spreading the intelligence, which fortunately reached some American shipmasters in time to save them. In October, 1793, as thirteen American vessels were in the port of Lisbon afraid to venture out, Church pleaded their case so vigorously that the Portuguese government agreed to give them an armed convoy. Nevertheless the Algerines found plenty of game among American ships then at sea, for they captured ten vessels and added one hundred and five more Americans to the stock of slaves in Algiers. "They are in a distressed and naked situation," wrote Captain O'Brien, who had himself then been eight years in captivity.

Humphreys made arrangements by which they received clothing and a money allowance ranging from twelve cents a day for a seaman up to eight dollars a month for a captain. Nothing, however, could be done in the way of peace negotiations. One of Humphreys' agents reported that the Dey could not make peace even if he really wanted to do so. "He declared to me that his interest does not permit him to accept your offers, Sir, even were you to lavish millions upon him, 'because,' said he, 'if I were to make peace with everybody, what should I do with my Corsairs? What should I do with my soldiers? They would take off my head, for want of other prizes.'"

This was an honest disclosure of the situation. Humphreys wrote Jefferson that "no choice is left for the United States but to prepare a naval force for the protection of their trade." Captain O'Brien wrote, "By all means urge Congress to fit out some remarkably fast sailing cruisers, well appointed and manned." In January, 1794, accordingly, a committee of the House brought in a resolution for building four ships of 44 guns and two of 20 guns each. The debate began on February 6, and for some time was altogether one-sided, with one speaker after another opposing the creation of a navy. Madison, as was now his habit, had doubts as to the propriety of the measure. He fancied that peace "might be purchased for less money than this armament would cost." Clark of New Jersey had "an objection to the establishment of a fleet, because, when once it had been commenced, there would be no end to it." He had "a scheme which he judged would be less expensive and more effectual. This was to hire the Portuguese to cruise against the Algerines." Baldwin of Georgia thought that "bribery alone could purchase security from the Algerines." Nicholas of Virginia "feared that we were not a match for the Algerines."

Smith of Maryland and Fitzsimmons of Pennsylvania championed the resolution, and Fisher Ames made some remarks on Madison's lack of spirit that caused Madison to define his position. He proposed as a substitute for the pending measure that money should "be employed in such a manner as should be found most effectual for obtaining a peace with the Regency of Algiers; and failing of this, that the sum should be applied to the end of obtaining protection from some of the European Powers." This motion warmed up the debate. Giles of Virginia came to Madison's support in a style that was not helpful. He "considered navies altogether as very foolish things. An immense quantity of property was

TRIBUTE TO THE ALGERINES 111

spread on the water for no purpose whatever, which might have been employed by land to the best purpose." The suggestion that the United States should be a hermit nation was an indiscreet exposure of the logical significance of Madison's plan, and it perhaps turned the scale in favor of employing force.

The bill came up in the House for final passage on March 10, 1794. Its opponents now sparred for time, but a motion to recommit in order to give opportunity for further consideration was defeated by 48 to 41. Giles made a final effort, by a long and elaborate address, in which he argued that the effect of fitting out a navy would be to involve the United States in war with all the European Powers. Moreover, a navy would be dangerous to American liberty. "A navy is the most expensive of all means of defense, and the tyranny of governments consists in the expensiveness of their machinery." He pointed to the results of British naval policy. "The government is not yet destroyed, but the people are oppressed, liberty is banished." The French monarchy had been ruined by its navy. He was "astonished, with these fatal examples before our eyes, that there should be gentlemen who would wish to enter upon this fashionable system of politics." In discussing the expense of maintaining a navy, he expressed his fear that it would eventually bring back the miseries of feudalism.

William Smith of South Carolina made a reply in which he defined the issue as being between defense and tribute; but Giles had the last word. He wanted to know whether it was maintained that the frigates it was proposed to build would "boldly march upon land and break the chains of the prisoners?" He begged Congress not to do what "would irritate the barbarians and furnish additional misery to the unfortunate prisoners." In this closing struggle over the bill Giles fought single-handed. When he had quite finished, the bill was passed by 50 yeas to 39 nays, a result which showed a decided gain in strength from the discussion.

The debates in the Senate have not been preserved, but the Senate was so evenly divided that it took the casting vote of the Vice-President to pass the bill, which became law March 27, 1794. In order to get it passed at all, a proviso had been tacked on that, if peace terms could be arranged, "no farther proceeding be had under this Act." In September, 1795, a treaty of peace with Algiers

TRIBUTE TO THE ALGERINES

was finally concluded, after negotiations had been facilitated by a contingent fee of $18,000 paid to "Bacri the Jew, who has as much art in this sort of management as any man we ever knew," the American agents reported. It was a keen bargain, as Bacri had to propitiate court officials at his own risk, and had to look for both reimbursement and personal profit, too, out of the lump sum he was to receive in event of his success. It can hardly be doubted that he had the situation securely in hand before making the bargain. The money paid in Algiers for the ransom of the captives, for tribute and for presents to officials amounted to $642,500.00. But in addition the United States agreed to build a frigate for the Algerine navy and also supply naval stores, which with incidental expenses brought the total cost of the peace treaty up to $992,463.25. Moreover, the United States agreed to pay an annual tribute of 12,000 sequins, —about $27,500.

By the terms of the navy act, the United States had to stop building vessels for its own protection. Of those which had been authorized, the frigates *Constitution*, *United States*, and *Constellation* were under way and were eventually completed. The timber, with material that had been collected for the other vessels, was sold, except what was needed for the frigate which was to be presented to the Algerines, and which was to be built at Portsmouth, N. H. The whole affair was a melancholy business that must have occasioned Washington deep chagrin. In his address to Congress, December 7, 1796, announcing the success of the negotiations for effecting the release of the captives, he observed that "to secure respect to a neutral flag requires a naval force, organized and ready to vindicate it from insult or aggression."

CHAPTER VI

FRENCH DESIGNS ON AMERICA

A FEW months before France declared war upon England, February 1, 1793, Edmond Genet was appointed French Minister to the United States. He landed at Charleston, April 8, and at once began activities so authoritative as to amount to an erection of French sovereignty in the United States. The subsequent failure of his efforts and the abrupt ending of his diplomatic career have so reacted upon his reputation that associations of boastful arrogance and reckless incompetency cling to his name. This estimate holds him too lightly and underrates the peril to which the United States was then exposed. Genet was no casual rhetorician raised to important office by caprice of events, but a trained diplomatist of hereditary aptitude and of long experience. His father was chief of the bureau of correspondence in the Department of Foreign Affairs for the French monarchy, and it was as an interpreter attached to that bureau that the son began his career in 1775. While still a youth, he gained literary distinction by his translations of historical works from Swedish into French. Genet was successively attached to the French Embassies at Berlin and Vienna, and in 1781 he succeeded his father in the Department of Foreign Affairs. In 1788, he was Secretary of the French Embassy at St. Petersburg, where his zeal for French Revolutionary principles so irritated the Empress Catherine that she characterized him as "a furious demagogue," and in 1792 he was forced to leave Russia. In the same year he was named Ambassador to Holland, and thence was soon transferred to the United States.

It is obvious that a man of such experience could not be ignorant of diplomatic forms and of international proprieties of behavior. If he pursued a course that has since seemed to be a marvel of truculence, the explanation should be sought in the circumstances of his mission more than in the nature of his personality. When the matter is considered from this standpoint, not only does one find that Genet's proceedings become consistent and intelligible, but one becomes deeply impressed

FRENCH DESIGNS ON AMERICA 117

with the magnitude of the peril then confronting the United States. Nothing less than American independence was at stake.

It should be borne in mind that France, in aiding America against England, had been pursuing her own ends. In August, 1787, the French government advised its American representative that it had observed with indifference the movements going on in the United States and would view the break-up of the Confederation without regret. "We have never pretended to make of America a useful ally; we have had no other object than to deprive Great Britain of that vast continent." But, now that war with England had broken out again, it was worth while making an effort to convert America into a useful ally. Jefferson, while Minister to Paris, had been sympathetic with the Revolutionary movement. In 1789, the English Ambassador reported to his government that Jefferson was much consulted by the leaders of the Third Estate. On the other hand, Gouverneur Morris, who was then living in Paris, sympathized frankly with the King. Nevertheless he was chosen to succeed Jefferson as the American Minister. In notifying him of the appointment, Washington let him know that there had been objections. "It was urged that in France you were considered as a favorer of the aristocracy, and unfriendly to its Revolution." Washington's reminder that it was his business to promote the interest of his own country did not have any apparent effect on Morris's behavior. He became the personal agent of Louis XVI, and he not only received and disbursed large sums on the King's account, but he also entered into plans for the King's flight from Paris. During the Reign of Terror which began in 1792, he behaved with an energy and an intrepidity honorable to him as a man; in general, however, his course tended to embroil and not to guard American interests.

In the face of the European coalition against revolutionary France, the principle of action was that announced by Danton, — "to dare, and to dare, and without end to dare." Genet therefore went on his mission to America keyed to measures which were audacious but which can hardly be described as reckless. By plunging heavily he might make a big winning; if he failed, he was hardly worse off than if he had not made the attempt. To draw the United States into the war as the ally of France was only one part of his mission. He was also planning to reëstablish the

French colonial empire, the loss of which was still an unhealed wound. Canada, Louisiana, and the Floridas were all in his mind. In Louisiana, France regarded conditions as being so favorable that Genet was instructed to make special efforts in that quarter. Spain, which had entered the coalition against republican France, held the lower Mississippi. Spain was therefore the common enemy of France and of the American settlements west of the mountains. Ought not then those two republican interests to work together to expel Spain and to seize Louisiana? Moreover, there was a belief, not without grounds, that the older States which formed the American union were indifferent to the needs and interests of the country west of the Alleghenies and would be more relieved than afflicted if it should take its destinies into its own hands. Such considerations animated a group of Americans in Paris, among whose prominent members were Thomas Paine, the pamphleteer, Joel Barlow, the poet, and Dr. James O'Fallon, a Revolutionary soldier now interested in Western land speculation. All were then ardent sympathizers with the French Revolution, and they entered heartily into the design of stirring up the Western country against Spain. The project attracted some frontier leaders, among them George Rogers Clark, famous for his successful campaigns against the hostile Indians and the British during the Revolutionary War. He was to lead a force of Western riflemen against the Spanish posts in Louisiana, and Genet brought with him blank brevets of officers up to the grade of captain for bestowal on the Indian chiefs who would coöperate. The expenses of the expedition were to be met by collections which Genet expected to make from the treasury of the United States on account of sums due to France.

The project of using the United States as a French base could claim legal rights under the treaties of 1778 between France and the United States. There were two treaties, both concluded on the same day. One, entitled a treaty of amity and commerce, was a mutual conveyance of privileges; it provided that the ships of war of each country should defend the vessels of the other country against all attacks that might occur while they were in company. Besides this right of convoy, each country had the right to use the ports of the other, either for ships of war or for privateers and their prizes, "nor shall such prizes be arrested or seized when they come to and enter the ports of either party; nor shall the searchers or other officers of those places search the same, or make any examination concerning the lawfulness of such prizes, but they may hoist sail at any time, and depart." All vessels of either country had the right to take refuge in the ports of the other, whether from stress of weather or pursuit of enemies, "and they shall be permitted to refresh and provide themselves at reasonable rates, with victuals and all things needful for the sustenance of their persons or reparation of their ships, and conveniency of their voyage; and they shall no ways be detained or hindered from returning out of the said ports or roads, but may remove and depart when and whither they please, without any let or hindrance." It was expressly provided that such hospitality should not be extended to vessels of an enemy of either country. The accompanying instrument, entitled a treaty of alliance, was a mutual guarantee of territorial possessions, "forever against all other powers." These broad rights and privileges were supplemented by the convention of 1788 on consular functions, which facilitated the organization of a consular jurisdiction competent to deal with cases arising from the treaties. There was still due to France on loans contracted during the Revolution a remainder of about $2,300,000 payable by instalments, subject to the proviso that "Congress and the United States" had "the liberty of freeing themselves by anticipated payments should the state of their finances admit." It was planned to get the United States to reciprocate the past favors of France by favoring her now, if not by direct payments of money, at least by acceptances which Genet could use in purchasing supplies. The fact that whatever in the way of money or accommodations was obtained in the United States would be used in business in that country was counted upon to facilitate the transaction.

These facts form the background against which Genet's activities should be viewed. He came with deliberate intent to rush the situation, and armed with all needful powers for that purpose, so far as the French government could confer them. According to a dispatch from Morris to the State Department, Genet "took with him three hundred blank commissions which he is to distribute to such as will fit out cruisers in our ports to prey on the British commerce."

At Charleston, Genet received an enthusiastic reception. The Revolutionary commander, Gen-

FRENCH DESIGNS ON AMERICA 123

eral Moultrie, who was then governor of South Carolina, entered so cordially into Genet's plans that in his first dispatch home, Genet was able to say to his government that Moultrie had permitted him to arm privateers and had assisted the various branches of his mission in every possible way. Such was Genet's energy that within five days after his arrival he had opened a recruiting station at which American seamen were taken into the French service; he had commissioned American vessels as French privateers; and he had turned the French consul's office into an admiralty court for which business was provided by the prizes that were being brought in.

After seeing under way all matters that he could attend to in Charleston, Genet moved on to Philadelphia, and received on his way thither such greetings as to give to his journey the character of a triumphal progress. Meanwhile, *L'Ambuscade*, the French frigate which had brought Genet to Charleston, was proceeding to Philadelphia, taking prizes on her way and sending them to American ports. In Delaware Bay she captured the *Grange*, an English merchantman lying there at anchor, and took this vessel with her to Philadelphia as a prize. As Genet neared Philadelphia on

May 16, *L'Ambuscade* gave notice by firing three guns, at which signal a procession was formed to meet Genet at Gray's Ferry and escort him to his lodgings. He found awaiting him a letter from George Rogers Clark, which gave an account of his plans for the invasion of Louisiana and the capture of New Orleans, and which announced his readiness to start if he were assisted by some frigates and provided with three thousand pounds sterling to meet expenses. Genet received reports from other agents or friendly correspondents in the Spanish territory, and so active was he in forwarding the objects of his mission that on June 19 he was able to write to his government, "I am provisioning the West Indies, I excite the Canadians to break the British yoke, I arm the Kentukois and prepare a naval expedition which will facilitate their descent on New Orleans."

These claims were well founded. Genet did, in fact, make an effective start, and had he been able to command funds he might have opened a great chapter of history. George Rogers Clark was the ablest and most successful commander that the frontier had yet produced, and such was the weakness of the Spanish defenses that had his expedition been actually launched as planned, the conquest of Louisiana might indeed have been accomplished. It was not any defect in Genet's arrangements that frustrated his plans, but his inability to raise money and the uncertainty of his position as the agent of a government which was undergoing rapid revolutionary change.

News that the French Republic had declared war against Great Britain reached the United States early in April, 1793. Washington, who was then at Mount Vernon, wrote to Jefferson that "it behooves the Government of this country to use every means in its power to prevent the citizens thereof from embroiling us with either of those Powers, by endeavoring to maintain a strict neutrality," and he requested that the Secretary should "give the subject mature consideration, that such measures as shall be deemed most likely to effect this desirable purpose may be adopted without delay." On arriving at Philadelphia a few days later, Washington was met by a distracted Cabinet. The great difficulty was the conflict of obligations. The United States had a treaty of alliance with France; it had a treaty of peace with Great Britain. The situation had become such that it could not sustain both relations at the same time. If the

126 WASHINGTON AND HIS COLLEAGUES

United States remained neutral, it would have to deny to France privileges conferred by the treaty which had been negotiated when both countries were at war with Great Britain. How far was that treaty now binding? It had been made with "the Most Christian king," whose head had been cut off. Did not his engagements fall with his head? That was the very position taken by the government of the French Republic, which had asserted the right to decide what treaties of the old monarchy should be retained and what rejected. As an incident of the present case, the question was to be decided whether the ambassador of the French Republic should be received.

Such were the issues that Washington's Administration had to face, at a time when the whole country was thrilling with enthusiasm in behalf of the French Republic. Chief Justice Marshall left on record his opinion that this feeling "was almost universal," and that "a great majority of the American people deemed it criminal to remain unconcerned spectators of a conflict between their ancient enemy and republican France."

Washington acted with his customary deliberation. On April 18, 1793, he submitted to the members of his Cabinet thirteen questions. Jefferson, who held that the French treaty was still operative, noted that the questions reached him in Washington's own handwriting, "yet it was palpable from the style, their ingenious tissue and suite, that they were not the President's, that they were raised upon a prepared chain of argument, in short, that the language was Hamilton's and the doubts his alone." In Jefferson's opinion they were designed to lead "to a declaration of the Executive that our treaty with France is void." Jefferson was right as to Hamilton's authorship. At a time when Jefferson had no advice to give save that it would be well to consider whether Congress ought not to be summoned, Hamilton had ready a set of interrogatories which subjected the whole situation to close analysis. The critical questions were these:

"Shall a proclamation issue for the purpose of preventing interferences of the citizens of the United States in the war between France and Great Britain, &c.? Shall it contain a declaration of neutrality or not? What shall it contain?

"Are the United States obliged, by good faith, to consider the treaties heretofore made with France as applying to the present situation of the parties? May they either renounce them, or hold them suspended till the government of France shall be established?"

To the interrogatories framed by Hamilton, Washington added one which presented the point raised by Jefferson—"Is it necessary or advisable to call together the two Houses of Congress, with a view to the present posture of European affairs? If it is, what shall be the particular object of such a call?"

The Cabinet met on April 19. On the question of a proclamation of neutrality Jefferson argued that such a proclamation would be equivalent to a declaration that the United States would not take part in the war, and that this matter did not lie within the power of the Executive, since it was the province of Congress to declare war. Congress ought therefore to be called to consider the question. Hamilton, who held that it was both the right and the duty of the President to proclaim neutrality, was strongly opposed to summoning Congress. In a brief record of the proceedings he remarked that "whether this advice proceeded from a secret wish to involve us in a war, or from a constitutional timidity, certain it is such a step would have been fatal to the peace and tranquillity of America." The matter was finally compro-

FRENCH DESIGNS ON AMERICA

mised by an unanimous agreement that a proclamation should be issued "forbidding our citizens taking any part in any hostilities on the seas with or against any of the belligerent powers; and warning them against carrying to any such powers any of those articles deemed contraband, according to the modern usage of nations; and enjoining them from all acts and proceedings inconsistent with the duties of a friendly nation toward those at war." Jefferson's scruples having been appeased by avoiding the use of the term "neutrality," it was now unanimously decided that Congress should not be called. It was further decided that the French Minister should be received. Jefferson and Randolph, however, were of opinion that he should be received without conditions, while Hamilton, supported by Knox, held that the Minister ought to be apprised of the intention to reserve the question whether the treaties were still operative; "lest silence on that point should occasion misconstruction." The even division of the Cabinet on this point was in practical effect a victory for Jefferson. The Cabinet was unable to reach any decision in the matter of treaty obligations. Jefferson held that they were still operative; Hamilton, that they were "temporarily and

130 WASHINGTON AND HIS COLLEAGUES

provisionally suspended." Knox sided with Hamilton, and Randolph, although he at first sided with Jefferson, was so shaken in his opinion by Hamilton's argument that he asked further time for consideration. Eventually written opinions were submitted by Hamilton, Jefferson, and Randolph, confirming the views they had previously expressed, and, as Knox concurred with Hamilton, the Cabinet was still evenly divided on that fundamental question.

The proclamation, on the lines upon which all had agreed, was draughted by Randolph who showed it to Jefferson in order to assure him that "there was no such word as neutrality in it." Jefferson, whose own account this is, did not mention that he raised any objection to the wording of the proclamation at the time, though a few months later he referred to it in his private correspondence as a piece of "pusillanimity," because it omitted any expression of the affection of America for France. The proclamation was issued on April 22, two weeks after the arrival of Genet at Charleston. The procedure that had been adopted at Jefferson's instance avoided none of the difficulties that a declaration of neutrality would have encountered but rather increased them by putting the

Government in a false position. The mere omission of the term did not prevent it from being known as a neutrality proclamation. It was at once so designated and has always been so considered. Jefferson himself, in advising the American foreign representatives of the policy of the Government, said that it would be "a fair neutrality"; and, in writing to Madison a few days after the proclamation had been issued, he remarked, "I fear a fair neutrality will prove a disagreeable pill to our friends, though necessary to keep us out of the calamities of war."

By its terms, however, the proclamation was simply an admonition to American citizens to keep out of the war, with notice that, if they got into trouble by engaging in contraband trade, they would not receive the protection of the United States, and would be liable to prosecution for the commission of acts of a nature to "violate the law of nations." It is manifest that the question whether or not the French treaty was still in operation was of great practical importance. If it was still in force, the treaty formed part of the law of the land, and American citizens might plead immunity for acts done in pursuance of its provisions. Hamilton was for suspending the treaty since a situation had arisen which made its provisions inconsistent with a policy of neutrality. His main contention was that the obligations imposed by the treaty of '78 were no longer binding on the United States, since they contemplated only defensive war. By her declaration of war France had taken the offensive, thereby relieving the United States of her reciprocal obligations. Jefferson held that the treaty was still operative, for even if its provisions apparently required the United States to engage in the war, it did not follow that such action would be an actual consequence. The possibility was "not yet certain enough to authorize us in sound morality to declare, at this moment, the treaties null."

Meanwhile Genet was left in a position in which he had a perfect right to claim all privileges conferred on France by the treaty. The result was a curious chapter of diplomatic correspondence. Genet took an attitude of indignant remonstrance at the duplicity of the American position. Did not the United States have a treaty with France? By what authority then did the Administration interfere with him in the enjoyment of his rights as the representative of France, and interfere with American citizens in their dealings with him?

He shrewdly refrained from any attempt to defend the capture of the *Grange* by *L'Ambuscade* in Delaware Bay. "The learned conclusions of the Attorney-General of the United States, and the declarations of the American Government, have been on this subject the rule of my conduct. I have caused the prize to be given up." But he stood firm on rights secured by the treaty. "As long as the States, assembled in Congress, shall not have determined that this solemn engagement should not be performed, no one has the right to shackle our operations, and to annul their effect, by hindering those of our marines who may be in the American ports, to take advantage of the commissions which the French Government has charged me to give to them, authorizing them to defend themselves, and fulfill, if they find an opportunity, all the duties of citizens against the enemies of the State."

This was using an argument borrowed from Jefferson's abundant stock of constitutional limitations. Genet was, of course, advised of the dissensions in the Cabinet. He was on such confidential terms with Jefferson that he talked freely about the projected raid on Louisiana. Jefferson noted in his diary that "he communicated these things to me, not as Secretary of State, but as Mr. Jefferson." Jefferson told Genet that he "did not care what insurrections should be excited in Louisiana," but that "enticing officers and soldiers from Kentucky to go against Spain was really putting a halter about their necks, for that they would assuredly be hung if they commenced hostilities against a nation at peace with the United States." So great is the force of legal pedantry that Jefferson was unable to agree that the President should proclaim neutrality in clear and positive terms; but that same pedantry was effectively employed in covering the legal flaws of Jefferson's position in his notes to Genet. He attenuated the treaty obligations by strict construction and also by reservations founded on the general principles of international law. "By our treaties with several of the belligerent Powers," he told Genet, "we have established a style of peace with them. But without appealing to treaties, we are at peace with them all by the law of nature: for, by nature's law, man is at peace with man." Hence the propriety of forbidding acts within American jurisdiction that would cause disturbance of this peace, a point on which he quoted copiously from Vattel. Genet manifested some irritation at being referred to treatises on international law when he was resting his case on a treaty the validity of which Jefferson acknowledged. "Let us not lower ourselves," he wrote, "to the level of ancient politics by diplomatic subtleties. Let us be frank in our overtures, in our declarations, as our two nations are in their affections, and, by this plain and sincere conduct, arrive at the object by the shortest way."

Logically Jefferson's position was that of maintaining the validity of the treaty while opposing the fulfillment of its obligations. At the same time he had to carry on a correspondence with Hammond, the British Minister, who was making complaints of the use of American ports for French depredations on British commerce, and to him Jefferson pleaded entire willingness to discharge in good faith the obligations of a neutral Power. It may seem as if Jefferson was attempting the impossible feat of trying to ride at one time two horses going in opposite directions, but such was his dexterity that in appearance he was largely successful. Meanwhile he contrived to throw on Hamilton and his adherents the blame for the feebleness and inconsistency of national policy. In letters to his Congressional lieutenants, Monroe in the Senate and Madison in the House, he la-

136 WASHINGTON AND HIS COLLEAGUES

mented "the anglophobia, secret antigallomany" that have "decided the complexion of our dispositions." He spoke scornfully of Randolph, whom he regarded as so irresolute that the votes in the Cabinet were "generally two and a half against one and a half," by which he meant that Hamilton and Knox stood together against Jefferson, while Randolph divided his influence between the two factions.

So inflamed was the state of public opinion that a rising against the Government seemed possible. In a letter written twenty years later, John Adams described "the terrorism excited by Genet, in 1793, when ten thousand people in the streets of Philadelphia, day after day, threatened to drag Washington out of his house, and effect a revolution in the Government, or compel it to declare war in favor of the French Revolution and against England." Adams related that he "judged it prudent and necessary to order chests of arms from the War Office" to be brought into his house to defend it from attack, and he had it from "the coolest and firmest minds" that nothing but the outbreak of yellow fever in Philadelphia that summer "could have saved the United States from a fatal revolution of government." On the other hand, letters written by Hamilton during the time of all this excitement show that he thought little of it, although he more than anyone else was its target. In May, 1793, he wrote that the number of persons who went to meet Genet "would be stated high at a hundred," and he did not believe that a tenth part of the city participated in the meetings and addresses of Genet's sympathizers. "A crowd will always draw a crowd, whatever be the purpose. Curiosity will supply the place of attachment to, or interest in, the object." Washington's own letters at this period show no trace of concern about his personal safety though he smarted under the attacks on his motives. An entry of August 2, 1793, in Jefferson's private diary, forming the volume since known as "The Anas," relates that at a cabinet meeting Knox exhibited a print entitled the funeral of George W——n, in which the President was placed on a guillotine. "The President was much inflamed; got into one of those passions when he cannot command himself; ran much on the personal abuse which had been bestowed upon him; defied any man on earth to produce one single act of his since he had been in the Government which was not done from the purest motives; that he had never repented but once the having slipped the moment of resigning his office, and that was every moment since; that by God he had rather be in his grave than in his present situation; that he had rather be on his farm than to be made emperor of the world; and that they were charging him with wanting to be king; that that rascal Freneau sent him three of his papers every day, as if he thought he would become the distributor of his papers; that he could see in this nothing but an impudent design to insult him."

Freneau was one of Jefferson's subordinates in the State Department, combining with his duties there the editorship of a newspaper engaged in spreading the calumny that the Administration was leaning toward monarchy through the influence of Hamilton and his friends, who despised republicanism, hated France, and loved England. This journalistic campaign went on under the protection of Jefferson to the disturbance of an administration of which Jefferson himself formed a part. This circumstance has given trouble to Jefferson's biographers, and it is now somewhat difficult to make those allowances to which Jefferson is entitled from the candid historian. Such behavior at the present day would be regarded as treacherous, for it is now a settled doctrine that it is the duty of a member of the President's Cabinet to give unreserved support to his policy, or to resign. But at that period, neither in England nor in the United States, did this view of cabinet solidarity prevail. It was not considered against the rules of the game for a cabinet official to use any opportunities within reach for promoting his aims or to boast such behavior as patriotic zeal. Jefferson, who wanted to resign and stayed on only at Washington's earnest desire, certainly rendered a service to the Administration, which was then so unpopular that Jefferson's connection with it was a political asset of great value.

Hamilton also made use of the services of journalism. When on June 29, 1793, publication began of a series of eight articles signed "Pacificus," it was well known that Hamilton was the author. The acute analysis and cogent reasoning of these articles have given them classic rank as an exposition of national rights and duties. Upon minds open to reason their effect was marked. Jefferson wrote to Madison, "For God's sake, my dear Sir, take up your pen, select the most striking heresies, and cut him to pieces in the face of the public." Madison did take up his pen, but he laid it down again without attempting to controvert Hamilton's argument. The five articles which Madison wrote over the signature "Helvidius" do not proceed farther into the subject than a preliminary examination of executive authority, in which he laid down principles of strict construction of the Constitution which have never been adopted in practice and which are now interesting only as specimens of dialectic subtlety.

Although as an electioneering tactician Jefferson had superior ability, neither he nor any of his associates was a match for Hamilton in debate. As the issues were discussed, the Jeffersonians lost ground, and for this they put the blame on Genet. By July 7, Jefferson was writing to Madison that Genet "renders my position immensely difficult," and thereafter in the correspondence of Jefferson, Madison, and Monroe, Genet figures as a rash man whose indiscretions embarrassed his friends and impeded his own objects. This view has to a large extent passed over into history, but when it is considered that Genet did not come to America for Jefferson's comfort but to accomplish certain things for his own government, it must be owned that he had considerable success. Although his means were small, he managed to engage in the French service an active American fleet including such vessels as *Le Cassius*, *L'Ami de le Point à Petre*, *L'Amour de la Liberté*, *La Vengeance*, *La Montagne*, *Le Vainqueur de la Bastille*, *La Carmagnole*, *L'Espérance*, *Le Citoyen Genet*, *Sans Pareil*, and *Le Petit Démocrate*. The last-mentioned vessel was originally an English merchantman, the brig *Little Sarah*, brought into Philadelphia harbor as a French prize. When it was learned that this vessel had been armed and equipped for service as a French man-of-war, Governor Mifflin of Pennsylvania gave orders that the vessel should be detained. Genet threatened forcible resistance, and a clash might have occurred, had Jefferson not intervened. He went to Genet's house on Sunday to persuade him not to move the vessel until the President could decide the case. Genet refused to give any promise, but remarked that the vessel would probably not be ready to depart for several days. Jefferson thereupon exerted himself successfully to prevent the taking of any steps to detain the vessel.

Washington, harassed and confused by the dissensions of his Cabinet, now desired that the advice of the justices of the Supreme Court be taken. Hamilton was opposed to a proceeding which involved prejudgment by the Court on questions which might come before it in due course of law, and which seemed to him also to be an avoidance of the proper responsibility of the executive. Nevertheless he took part in preparing the case, and of the twenty-nine questions submitted to the Supreme Court, Hamilton framed twenty-one, Jefferson seven, and Washington himself the last. Jefferson notified Genet of this consultation as an additional reason for patience, "the object of it being to obtain the best advice possible on the sense of the laws and treaties respecting the several cases. I am persuaded you will think the delay well compensated." Genet did not think so, and *Le Petit Démocrate* put to sea in defiance of American authority.

The justices declined to answer the questions, and the Administration had to face its responsibilities on its own judgment of its rights and duties. At least one member of the Administration had clear and positive ideas on that subject. Hamilton, who in his "Pacificus" letters had given a masterly exposition of international obligations, now took up the particular issues raised by Genet's claims, which at that time were receiving ardent championship. Freneau's *National Gazette* held that Genet had really acted "too tamely," had been "too accommodating for the peace of the United States." Hamilton now replied by a series of articles in the *Daily Advertiser* over the signature "No Jacobin," in which Genet's behavior was reviewed. After five articles had appeared in rapid succession, the series was abruptly terminated because Hamilton was taken down by the yellow fever.

The journalistic war was almost in the nature of a duel between the State and the Treasury Departments. Genet must have been amused. Lack of funds hindered his activities more than anything else. Jefferson had advised Washington that, "if the instalments falling due in this year could be advanced without incurring more danger," it would be well to make the payments, as he "thought it very material to keep alive the friendly sentiments of France." But this was a matter which pertained to Hamilton's own department, and in that field his advice controlled Washington. Genet could do nothing in this direction, and before the affair of *Le Petit Démocrate* he had ceased to expect financial aid.

Jefferson was now so angry and indignant that he no longer opposed the suggestions that had been made in cabinet meetings that Genet should be dismissed, and the note on that subject which he drafted for transmission to the French Government is an able document. The French Government, with ample reason, conditioned the recall of Genet upon the recall of Morris, who was succeeded by James Monroe. Meanwhile Genet's situation had become perilous through revolution at home. On October 16, 1793, his Government issued an order for his arrest. The United States now became his asylum. He acquired citizenship, married a daughter of Governor Clinton of New York, and settled down to a useful and respected career as a country gentleman devoted to the improvement of agriculture. He died at his home, Schodak, New York, in 1834, after having founded an American family.

At the time when Genet, favored by the exasperated state of Western sentiment over the navigation of the lower Mississippi, was promoting an attack upon the Spanish posts, the Administration had already been engaged for a long time in efforts to secure "full enjoyment of that navigation," as well as a settlement of the southwestern boundary. In December, 1791, Washington nominated William Carmichael, chargé d'affaires in Spain, and William Short, then chargé d'affaires

FRENCH DESIGNS ON AMERICA 145

in France, commissioners to make a treaty. Their efforts proved unsuccessful, and in 1794 the Spanish commissioner in the United States gave notice that they were not acceptable personally, and that it "was hoped that some other person would be appointed, with full powers, to settle this treaty, and graced with such a character as became the royalty to which he was accredited." Washington then nominated Thomas Pinckney, at that time minister in London, as minister plenipotentiary in Spain. When Pinckney arrived on the scene he was met with the dilatory methods then characteristic of Spanish diplomacy, and finally he had to bring matters to an issue by demanding his passports. His determination so impressed the Spanish Government that it finally consented to a treaty, October 27, 1795, which fixed the southern boundary of the United States and opened the Mississippi River to navigation. The boundary line was to run east along the thirty-first parallel of latitude from the Mississippi to the Appalachicola, thence along the latter river to its junction with the Flint, thence to the headwaters of the St. Mary's, and along its course to the Atlantic Ocean. The free navigation of the Mississippi was coupled with the privilege of depositing merchandise at New Orleans "without paying any other duty than a fair price for the hire of the stores." This privilege was to be continued after three years, or "an equivalent establishment" on the banks of the Mississippi was to be assigned to citizens of the United States — a provision which was not free from ambiguities and which furnished fresh material for controversy a few years later.

CHAPTER VII

A SETTLEMENT WITH ENGLAND

ACCORDING to Jefferson, the President originally took the same view of the French treaty that he did. Jefferson relates that on April 18, 1793, Washington spoke of having "never had a doubt of the validity of the French treaty," and he notes that in the cabinet disputes Washington was inclined to his views. As the embarrassments of the Administration thickened, the President, it is true, leaned more and more toward Hamilton, but this inclination was due more to necessity than to personal partiality. The explanation stands out in Jefferson's own account of events. Hamilton was clear, positive, and decided as to what to do and how to do it. Jefferson was active in finding objections but not in finding ways and means of action. This contrast became sharper as time went on, and, as Washington was in a position where he had to do something, he was forced to rely on Hamilton more and more. Jefferson held that it would be inexpedient for the general government to assume the duty of fortifying the harbors, and that there was no constitutional authority for establishing a military academy. On November 28, 1793, there was a prolonged wrangle over these issues at a cabinet meeting, which the President ended by saying that he would recommend the military academy to Congress, and "let them decide for themselves whether the Constitution authorized it or not." This was the last of the quarrelsome cabinet sessions recorded by Jefferson. He vacated the office of Secretary of State, December 31, 1793, and thereafter the ascendancy of Hamilton in the Cabinet was indisputed.

An immediate effect of the change was to give new vigor to efforts at reaching a settlement with Great Britain. The old troubles over her retention of the western posts still continued, and in addition to them came new difficulties arising from war measures. On January 30, 1793, Thomas Pinckney, then American minister to Great Britain, wrote that war was about to begin, "and although our claim to a free intercourse is founded in reason and our national right, yet, as we have no armed

A SETTLEMENT WITH ENGLAND 149

neutrality the members whereof this people have to fear, they may stop our vessels bound to French ports with provisions." What was feared soon happened. By the French decree of 1793, the French colonies were opened to American trade and West Indian commerce flourished. This was now afflicted by contraband regulations laid down by Great Britain, under which many American vessels were seized for carrying cargoes to or from French ports. Although Genet's activities and the extent to which they were indulged by the United States did not tend to promote friendly relations with Great Britain, yet it does not appear that the British policy was inspired by resentment. The regulations as defined by instructions issued on June 8, 1793, made liable to detention all vessels carrying "corn, flour, or meal" to French ports, with the proviso that the cargoes might be purchased on behalf of the British government and the ships might then be released with a due allowance for freight, or they might be allowed to dispose of their cargoes in the ports of any country in amity with Great Britain. Vessels attempting to enter a blockaded port were liable to seizure and condemnation, save that the ships of Denmark and Sweden might be seized only if they should persist in trying to enter after once having been turned back.

Conciliatory explanations were made by Hammond, the British minister, in notifying our State Department. He pointed out that only corn and flour were contraband, that the regulations did not extend to other provisions, and that they secured "to the proprietors, supposing them neutral, a full indemnification for any loss they may possibly sustain." The special privilege extended to Denmark and Sweden was attributed to treaty requirements and therefore could not be regarded as invidious. In reply Jefferson at home and Pinckney abroad argued in behalf of the United States for the principle that free ships make free goods, but Great Britain would not hearken to a doctrine that struck at the efficacy of her sea power.

Washington besought Congress to support the efforts of the Administration by making, for the defense of American interests, such provision as would inspire respect. In his address of December 3, 1793, he observed: "There is a rank due to the United States among nations which will be withheld, if not absolutely lost, by the reputation of weakness. If we desire to avoid insult, we must be able to repel it; if we desire to secure peace, one of

A SETTLEMENT WITH ENGLAND 151

the most powerful instruments of our rising prosperity, it must be known that we are at all times ready for war." The answer of Congress was the grudging consent to some naval preparations already recounted.

After the passage of the navy bill Sedgwick of Massachusetts endeavored to interest the House in the general subject of military preparation. On March 12, 1794, he introduced resolutions for raising fifteen additional regiments for two years, the term to be extended for three years in case of the outbreak of war. In advocating this measure he spoke of the sorry experience of the country in depending upon militia. Their "want of discipline occasions them to commit a great waste on the property of their fellow citizens, besides a waste of public property." As long as we depend upon militia, "European nations will not consider us as able to retaliate and assert our rights." Nothing came of this sensible proposal, but Sedgwick made an auxiliary suggestion which Congress did adopt. He urged that the sailing of vessels from the ports of the United States be prohibited. An embargo would hold over foreign nations the threat that, unless they behaved themselves, their supplies from the United States might be

152 WASHINGTON AND HIS COLLEAGUES

cut off. Such embargo was voted for a month from March 26, 1794, which was subsequently extended for another month, and the President was authorized to lay, regulate, and revoke embargoes during the recess of Congress. Congress regarded the embargo policy as a cheap way out of a difficult situation, but this method was really not only far more costly to the nation than would have been the straightforward course of arming for defense, but at the same time accomplished nothing. Dayton of New Jersey proposed to supplement the embargo by the sequestration of all debts due from citizens of the United States to British subjects. Clark of New Jersey outdid his colleague by proposing to prohibit all commercial intercourse between the United States and Great Britain until such time as that country should surrender the western posts and should make restitution for all losses sustained by American citizens.

Violent speeches were made on these proposals at the very time when the House was refusing to support either an army or a navy. Sedgwick introduced some good sense into a debate that was alternating between blatant vaporing and legal pedantry, by pointing out that, under the Constitution, the President of the United States ought

A SETTLEMENT WITH ENGLAND 153

to be allowed to have some say about the matter. It was the function of the President to treat with foreign powers, and yet the House was now considering action which was in effect "prescribing the terms of treaty, and restraining the constitutional power from treating on any other terms." This argument was used effectively by a number of speakers. It turned the main position taken by the advocates of non-intercourse, which was that the real objection came from the bondholders who feared that the ensuing loss of revenue might prevent them from getting their interest. Such imputations of sordid motive became fruitless when the issue was raised of the constitutional authority of the President, but the advocates of non-intercourse met this new point of view by pointing out that the Constitution gave Congress the right to regulate commerce. The feeling against Great Britain was so great that the House was bent on indulging it, and on April 25, 1794, the non-intercourse bill was passed by a vote of 58 to 34. The Senate was so evenly divided that, on the motion to pass the bill to its third reading, there was a tie vote, and Vice-President Adams, who was called upon for a casting vote, gave it against the bill. About a month later in the House another attempt was made to carry the policy of non-intercourse by a joint resolution, but by this time a reaction in favor of the Administration had set in and the resolution received only 24 yeas to 46 nays, James Madison being among those who stuck to the proposal to the last.

While the House was abandoning itself to reckless mischief-making, Washington was striving to arrange matters by negotiation. The perplexities of his situation were great and varied. As a military man he knew that American jurisdiction was precarious so long as Great Britain held the interior. The matter had been the subject of prolix correspondence between Jefferson and Hammond, but the American demands that Great Britain should surrender the frontier posts in accordance with the treaty of peace had been met by demands that America, in accordance with that same treaty, should first satisfy various claims of British subjects for restitution, indemnity, and relief. The regular diplomatic machinery stuck fast at this point, both at home and abroad. In one of his gossipy, confidential letters Fisher Ames remarked that Hammond was a most "petulant, impudent" man, habitually railing against the conduct of our government "with a

A SETTLEMENT WITH ENGLAND 155

gabble that his feelings render doubly unintelligible." But Pinckney, our representative in England, was equally undiplomatic. He was "sour and also Gallican"; although calm in manner, "he had prejudices, and unless a man has a mind above them, he can do little service there."

Washington decided that it would be wise to send a special envoy to deal with all the points at issue. He thought first of Hamilton, but was warned that the Senate would not ratify such an appointment. Hamilton recommended John Jay as "the only man in whose qualifications for success there would be thorough confidence." Jay was then chief-justice, but the crisis was so dangerous as to justify Washington in calling him even from that important post. He had matchless qualifications for the mission. He had been minister to Spain, 1778–1782; he had been one of the commissioners who had negotiated the treaty of peace of 1783; he had been Secretary of Foreign Affairs, 1784–1789; so that he had had an experience which familiarized him with every detail of the questions at issue. As a negotiator he had always gained marked success by acting upon his own principle that "a little good-natured wisdom often does more in politics than much slippery craft." Jay showed fine patriotism in accepting the appointment. He remarked to his friends that no man could frame a treaty with Great Britain without making himself unpopular and odious, and he accepted the mission under "a conviction that to refuse it would be to desert my duty for the sake of my ease and domestic concerns and comforts."

Jay was nominated as envoy extraordinary on April 16, 1794, and, after three days of violent debate, the appointment was confirmed by the Senate. The event did not moderate the rage of the House for immediate action. Some members urged that it was indelicate for the House to be passing reprisals at a time when the Executive was attempting friendly negotiations; but the reply was made that, if there was any indelicacy, it was on the part of the Executive, inasmuch as the House proceedings had been already begun when the President decided to nominate an envoy extraordinary. While Congress was fuming and wrangling, Jay was proceeding with his difficult task. He sailed on May 12, and on June 8 landed in England where he was hospitably received. Despite these personal attentions, the differences to be adjusted were so numerous and complicated that

A SETTLEMENT WITH ENGLAND 157

on the surface the situation looked almost hopeless. Conditions, however, were really more favorable than they appeared to be. A change, latent but influential, had taken place in the mental attitude of the governing class in England. There had been a notion that American independence would not last long and that the country would eventually be restored to the British Crown. The drift of events was rather in that direction until Hamilton's measures gave the ascendancy to the forces making for American national development. The practical statesmanship of Great Britain perhaps saw more clearly the significance of what was taking place than did that of America itself, and it was prepared to reckon with this new condition. Moreover, the European commotion resulting from the French Revolution had brought to the front a new set of interests and anxieties, for the free handling of which a settlement of differences with the United States might be advantageous. The effect of such considerations was at least to render the situation more manageable than might have been expected, and Jay improved his opportunities with admirable tact.

In pursuance of his principle of bringing "good-

158 WASHINGTON AND HIS COLLEAGUES

natured wisdom" to bear, Jay suggested to Lord Grenville, the British Secretary for Foreign Affairs, that they should dispense with written communications, and merely meet and converse informally "until there should appear a probability of coming to some amicable mutual understanding." Even after such understanding should be put into writing, it was not to be regarded as official or binding, but simply as an exchange of private memoranda. So strictly was this informal method adhered to that the regular force of secretaries and copyists had nothing to do with the proceedings until the treaty was almost ready for signing. Jay had been instructed to demand compensation for some three thousand slaves who had followed the British troops when they departed, but Lord Grenville stood firm on the principle that the slave, once under the British flag, became a free man, the property rights of the former owner thereupon becoming extinct and not forming a subject for compensation. Jay, who really held the same opinion, had to yield the point. It was agreed that the western posts should be evacuated by June 1, 1796, an arrangement which would allow the British government to retain them about two years longer. That government had already

A SETTLEMENT WITH ENGLAND 159

justified its retention of these posts by averring that the United States had not complied with the articles of the peace treaty relating to British debts. Jay was not in a position to argue the point with any force, for when he was Secretary of Foreign Affairs he had advised Congress that these articles "have been constantly violated on our part by legislative acts, then and still existing and operating"; and that Great Britain was therefore not to blame for retaining the posts. The British government was undoubtedly cognizant of this report, and Jay could not make any effective opposition to a proviso which in effect said to the United States, "before surrendering the posts we will wait and see whether you intend to fulfill your agreements." The root of the trouble — an evil often felt and still experienced in the United States — was defective sovereignty, an inability of the whole to control the behavior of its parts. Jay could not deny that the peace treaty had been violated by state legislation, and only by the humiliating means of an avowal of its impotence could he exonerate the national government from the imputation of bad faith. The matter was disposed of by provision for a joint commission to decide upon all cases in which it was alleged that unlawful impediments had been placed in the way of collection of debts due British subjects, and by the United States undertaking payment of the awards. A similar commission was to pass upon American claims for British violation of neutral rights. This arrangement was a concession whose practical value was eventually shown by the fact that as a result American merchants received some millions of dollars.

Jay displayed marked adroitness as a negotiator in dealing with the issues growing out of past differences, but he made an extraordinary slip in providing for commercial relations between the two countries. In their general tenor the articles displayed broad liberality. Between all British dominions in Europe and the territories of the United States there was to be "a reciprocal and perfect liberty of commerce and navigation." American vessels were to "be admitted and hospitably received" in the ports of East India, and, although participation in the coasting trade was prohibited, it was provided that this restriction should not prevent ships going from one port of discharge to another. The East Indian trade was not, however, so important as the nearer West Indian trade, and with respect to the latter

A SETTLEMENT WITH ENGLAND 161

the treaty provisions were narrow and exacting. American vessels were limited to seventy tons burden, and it was provided that "the United States will prohibit and restrain the carrying away of molasses, sugar, coffee, or cotton in American vessels, either for his Majesty's Islands or the United States, to any part of the world except the United States, reasonable sea-stores excepted." Jay, in a letter to Washington, excused his acceptance of this restraint on the ground that "the commercial part of the treaty may be terminated at the expiration of two years after the war, and in the meantime a state of things more auspicious to negotiation will probably arise, especially if the next session of Congress should not interpose fresh obstacles."

The treaty was silent on the subject of impressment, but Jay's failure on that point was just what was to have been expected in view of the unwillingness of the United States to defend its commerce. Impressment was not abandoned until many years afterwards, and then not through treaty stipulation but because the United States had a navy and could resist aggression on the seas. In its treatment of the subject of contraband, the treaty took positions in accord with the international law then received, but in one respect it made a distinct advance. Provision was made that war between the two countries should never become the pretext for confiscation of debts or annulment of contracts. This position involves the noble principle that war should never supersede justice but should be the servant of justice. Great practical advantage was experienced from it in the War of 1812, when the United States was a creditor nation.

On the whole, Jay's diplomacy was as enlightened as it was shrewd, but at the time it exposed him to furious denunciation which he disdained to notice. "I had read the history of Greece," he wrote to a friend, "and was apprised of the politics and proceedings of more recent date." The philosophic composure which he drew from his knowledge of history enabled him to behave with calm dignity while he was being burned in effigy, and while mob orators were heaping insult and calumny on his name. After a struggle that shook the Government, the treaty was ratified by the Senate on June 24, 1795, with the exception of the article about the West Indian trade, an omission to which Great Britain made no objection. The treaty was extremely unpopular, chiefly because

A SETTLEMENT WITH ENGLAND 163

unreasonable expectations of its provisions had been entertained. People had yet to learn that national independence has its defects as well as its advantages, and that the traditional intimacy between the West Indies and America was now on a footing of privilege and not of right. The great benefits conferred by the treaty were therefore not appreciated, and so violent was the fury its terms excited that it was perhaps fortunate that Jay did not resume his seat on the Supreme Bench. Before his return from England and before the details of the treaty had been made public, he had been elected governor of New York, and to accept this office he resigned the chief-justiceship.

CHAPTER VIII

PARTY VIOLENCE

WHEN, in July, 1793, Jefferson notified the President of his wish to resign from the Cabinet, Hamilton's resignation had already been before the President for several weeks. Ever since the removal of Congress to Philadelphia, Hamilton's circumstances had become less and less able to endure the strain of maintaining his official position on a salary of $3500 a year. He had fully experienced the truth of the warnings he had received that, if he gave himself to the public service, he might spend his time and substance without receiving gratitude for his efforts or credit for his motives. His vocation for statesmanship, however, was too genuine and his courage too high for such results to dishearten him. He had now accomplished what he had set out to do in securing the adoption of the measures which established the new government, and he no longer regarded his administrative position as essential to the success of his policy. Meanwhile the need had become urgent that he should resume the practice of his profession to provide for his family. It was not in his nature, however, to leave the front when a battle was coming on, and, although he gave early notice of his intention so that Washington should have ample time to look about for his successor, the resignation was not to become effective until Congress had met and shown its temper. According to Jefferson, Washington once remarked to him that he supposed Hamilton "had fixed on the latter part of next session to give an opportunity to Congress to examine into his conduct." Although Hamilton had made up his mind to retire, he intended to march out with flying colors, as became the victor on a hard-fought field. So far, he had met and beaten all enemies who had dared to assail his honor; he meant to beat them again if they renewed the attack, and he had word that one encounter was coming more formidable than any before.

Hamilton's success in carrying his measures through Congress, by sheer dexterity of management when numbers were against him, added intense bitterness to the natural chagrin felt by the defeated faction. Men like Jefferson and Madison were subject to traditions of behavior that required them to maintain a certain style of public decorum no matter how they might rage in private. But new men with new manners were coming on the scene, and among them the opposition to Hamilton had found a new leader — William Branch Giles of Virginia. He was a Princeton graduate of the class of 1781, had studied for the bar, and had been admitted to practice in 1786. To the full legal equipment of the period he added an energy and an audacity that speedily brought him legal and political distinction. He was active and outspoken in advocating the adoption of the new Constitution, at a time when popular sentiment in Virginia was strongly inclined to be adverse. He had no hesitation about undertaking unpopular causes, and hence British debt cases became a marked feature of his practice. Virginia State law had suspended the recovery of debts due British subjects until reparation had been made for the loss of negro slaves taken away by the British during the war, and until the western posts had been surrendered. But the peace treaty of 1783 stipulated that creditors on neither side should meet with lawful impediment

PARTY VIOLENCE 167

in the recovery of debts, and by the new Constitution treaties had become part of the law of the land. On the basis of a national jurisdiction in conflict with the Virginia statutes, Giles acted so energetically, that he himself related that by 1792 he had been employed in at least one hundred British debt cases, and was "as successful in collecting monies under judgments as is usually the case with citizens."

Comprehension of the true nature of the struggle in which Giles became conspicuous must start with the fact that the Constitution was reluctantly accepted and with great uneasiness as to possible consequences. In the Virginia convention of 1788, it was declared that the new Constitution was essentially a scheme of the military men to subject the people to their rule. This argument was not so much met as avoided by the declaration that there could be no tyranny while Washington lived. The rejoinder was obvious: what if he should not be able to withstand military influence? What if, in spite of him, the government should be given a dangerous character that would develop after he passed away? Jefferson had felt misgivings on this score from the first, and Madison experienced them as soon as differences on practical measures arose between himself and Hamilton. Jefferson and Madison wanted the government to be made respectable but not strong. Hamilton saw what they could not see — and indeed what few at that time could see — that a government cannot be made respectable without being made strong.

Washington was probably without any clear views of his own on constitutional questions, and what evidence there is on this point supports Jefferson's claim that Washington was more disposed to confide in him and in Madison than in Hamilton. When Jefferson relinquished the State Department, Washington proposed to give Madison the post, but was told he would not think of taking it. Washington then transferred Randolph to the position because he could not get anybody else of suitable capacity. Whatever Washington's personal inclinations may have been, he was in a position in which he had to act. Hamilton was the only one whom he could find to show him the way, and thus circumstances more and more compelled Washington to accept Hamilton's guidance, while at the same time it seemed increasingly clear to the opposition that it was above all things necessary to crush Hamilton. This state of sentiment must be kept in mind in order to make intelligible the rabid violence of the party warfare which had long been going on against Hamilton, and which — now that Jefferson had left the Cabinet — was soon to be extended to Washington himself.

When Giles went to the front in this war, both Jefferson and Madison were busy behind the firing line supplying munitions. Giles was elected in 1790 to fill a vacancy caused by the death of Theodorick Bland, and took his seat in the third session of the First Congress. The assumption bill had been passed, but that was only the first of the series of financial measures proposed by Hamilton, and Giles followed Madison's lead in unsuccessful resistance to the excise and to the national bank. Giles was re-elected to the Second Congress, which opened on October 24, 1791. In the course of this session he became the leader of the opposition, not by supplanting Madison but through willingness to take responsibilities from which Madison, like Jefferson, shrank, because he, too, preferred activity behind the scenes. This situation has often occurred in parliamentary history — a zealous party champion scouting the scruples and restraints that hampered the official leadership, and assuming an independent line of attack with the covert favor and assistance of that leadership. In the effort to crush Hamilton a series of raids was led by Giles, whose appetite for fighting could never be extinguished no matter how severe might be his defeat.

After much preliminary skirmishing which put heavy tasks on Hamilton in the way of getting up reports and documents, a grand attack was made on January 23, 1793. A series of resolutions, in drafting which Madison and Jefferson took part, was presented, calling for minute particulars of all loans, names of all persons to whom payments had been made, statements of semi-monthly balances between the Treasury and the Bank, and an account of the sinking fund and of unexpended appropriations, — all from the beginning of the government until the end of 1792. The resolution required Hamilton to complete and state all the accounts of the Treasury Department up to a period only a little over three weeks before the resolutions were presented, and to give a detailed transcript of particulars. But the Treasury accounts were in such perfect order, and so great was Hamilton's capacity for work, that the information called for was promptly transmitted in reports dated February 4, February 13, and February 14. At the same time Hamilton hit back by observing that the resolutions "were not moved without a pretty copious display of the reasons on which they were founded," which "were of a nature to excite attention, to beget alarm, to inspire doubts."

Giles was soon able to renew the attack. Jefferson and Madison helped him to prepare a series of nine resolutions which were presented on February 27. They specifically charged Hamilton with violation of law, neglect of duty, transgression of the proper limits of his authority, and indecorum in his attitude towards the House. The series ended with a resolution that a copy should be transmitted to the President. The proceeding was a sort of impeachment, framed with the purpose not of bringing Hamilton to trial but of forcing him out of the Cabinet. The charges against him were purely technical and were actuated by malevolence. Hamilton, though not allowed to come into the House to defend himself, nevertheless participated in the debate indirectly by writing the speech delivered by William Smith and credited to him in the Annals of Congress. It was so generally felt in Congress that the resolutions were founded on nothing more substantial than spite that Giles could not hold his forces together, and as the debate proceeded the number of his adherents dwindled. The House began voting at a night session on March 1st. After the third resolution had been defeated by a vote of 40 to 12, an attempt was made to withdraw the others, but such action was refused, and one by one the remaining resolutions were defeated by increasing numbers until only seven voted with Giles at the last, among them James Madison. It was a signal triumph for Hamilton. But his enemies were not disposed to accept the decision as final, and Jefferson thought it might be revised at the next session.

It was not until the Second Congress that the old factions finally disappeared and the formation of national parties began. The issue over the adoption of the Constitution had produced Federalists and Anti-Federalists, but with its adoption Anti-Federalism as such became a thing of the past. Opposition to the Government had to betake itself to the political platform provided by the successful introduction of the new system of government, and was obliged to distinguish itself from official Federalism by attacking not the Constitution but the way in which the Constitution was being construed and applied. The suspicion, jealousy, and dislike with which the new government was regarded in many quarters were reflected from the beginning in the behavior of Congress. There was from the first a disposition to find fault and to antagonize, and as time went on this disposition was aggravated by the great scope allowed to misunderstanding and calumny from the lack of direct contact between Congress and the Administration. In founding a new party, Jefferson only organized forces that were demanding leadership. He consolidated the existing opposition, and gave it the name "Republican Party," implying that its purpose was to resist the rise of monarchy and the growth of royal prerogative in the system of government which was introduced by the adoption of the Constitution. It is clear enough now that the implication was mere calumny; the notion that Washington was either aiming at monarchy or was conniving at it through ignorance was a grotesque travesty of the shameful situation that actually existed; but fictions, pretenses, slanders, and calumnies that would never have been allowed utterance if the Administration and Congress had stood face to face now had opportunity to spread and infect public opinion. Hence the tone of extreme rage that dishonors the political contention of the period and the malice that stains the correspondence of the faction chiefs.

Although a distinct party opposition appeared and assumed a name during the Second Congress, it disavowed as yet any opposition to Washington and represented its actual attempts to thwart the measures of the Administration as efforts to counteract Washington's evil advisers. The old constitutional tradition that the king can do no wrong, which still lingered in American politics, tended to an analogous elevation of the presidential office above the field of party strife, while leaving the President's Cabinet advisers fully exposed to it, just as in the case of the ministers of the Crown in England. Allowance must be made for the effect of this tradition when judgment is passed on the political activities of the period. Considered with regard to present standards of political behavior, the course of Jefferson in fomenting opposition to the Administration of which he was a part wears the appearance of despicable intrigue. There was nothing mean or low about it, however, in the opinion of himself and his friends, and even his enemies would have allowed it to be within the rules of the game. Jefferson did his best to defeat in Congress measures adopted by Washington on the advice of Hamilton, and he also did his best to undermine Washington's confidence in Hamilton. In his personal dealings with Washington, Jefferson had every advantage, for he had Washington's ear and could, more readily than Hamilton, direct the currents of unconscious influence that produce the will to believe. But Jefferson's animosity kept tempting him to overplay his hand in a way that was fatal in the face of an antagonist so keen and so dexterous as Hamilton.

In a letter of May 23, 1792, Jefferson presented to Washington an elaborate indictment of Hamilton's policy as a justification of his own behavior in organizing an opposition party in Congress. He charged Hamilton with subverting the character of the Government by his financial measures, the logical consequence of which would be "a change from the present republican form of government to that of a monarchy." Hence the need for organizing "the Republican party who wish to preserve the government in its present form." Washington thought over the matter, and — according to Jefferson — reopened the subject in a personal interview on July 10. Being now fully apprised of Jefferson's case, Washington himself prepared a brief of it, divided into numbered sections, and applied to Hamilton for a statement of his ideas upon the "enumerated discontents," framed so "that those ideas may be applied to the correspondent numbers." The proceeding is a fine instance of the care which Washington exercised in forming his opinions. Of course, as soon as charges of corruption and misdemeanor were reduced to exact statement the matter was put just where Hamilton wanted to get it, and in the grasp of his powerful hands its trashy character was promptly displayed. It is needless to go into details, now that public loans, the funding of floating indebtedness in excess of current income, and the maintenance of a national banking system to supply machinery of credit, are such well recognized functions that the wonder is how any statesman could have ever thought otherwise. Jefferson's arguments, when read with the prepossessions of the present day, are so apt to leave an impression of absurdity that they constitute a troublesome episode for his biographers.

Jefferson's maneuvering utterly failed to injure Hamilton in Washington's esteem, but it did have the effect of so thoroughly disgusting Washington with public life that at one time he was determined to refuse a reëlection, and even went so far as to ask Madison to prepare a valedictory address for him. He consented to serve another term most reluctantly, and not until he had been besought to do so by the leaders on both sides. Jefferson was as urgent as was Hamilton. While Washington was still wavering, he received a strong letter from Edmund Randolph that doubtless touched his soldierly pride. The letter closed with this sharp argument:

"You suffered yourself to yield when the voice of your country summoned you to the Administration. Should a civil war arise, you cannot stay at home. And how much easier will it be to disperse the factions, which are rushing to this catastrophe, than to subdue them after they shall appear in arms? It is the fixed opinion of the world, that you surrender nothing incomplete."

An appeal of this character was the most effective that could possibly be addressed to Washington, but in consenting he grumbled over the hardship of having to keep in active service at his time of life after already having served for so long a time. He complained that his hearing was getting bad and that "perhaps his other faculties might fall off and he not be sensible of it."

178 WASHINGTON AND HIS COLLEAGUES

Acquiescence in Washington's candidacy made it practically impossible for the Republican party to manifest its true strength. The compliment of Republican support was awarded to Governor Clinton of New York, who together with Washington received all the electoral votes of Virginia, New York, North Carolina, and Georgia. A stray electoral vote from Pennsylvania brought Clinton's total up to 50, whereas John Adams received 77 votes which re-elected him as vice-president. Jefferson received only four electoral votes, all from Kentucky, but his poor showing in this election was wholly due to the intricacy of the electoral system, and his party meanwhile developed so much strength that when the Third Congress met on December 2, 1793, the Republicans were strong enough to elect the speaker.

Undeterred by this circumstance, Hamilton forced the fighting. The Jeffersonians had been excusing the defeat they had received in attacking Hamilton in the previous Congress on the ground that the House had acted without allowing sufficient time for due examination of the evidence. This plea supplied to Hamilton an occasion for prompt action. Exactly two weeks after the meeting of Congress he addressed a letter to the

PARTY VIOLENCE 179

Speaker, in which he declared: "Unwilling to leave the matter on such a footing, I have concluded to request of the House of Representatives, as I now do, that a new inquiry may be, without delay, instituted in some mode, most effectual for an accurate and thorough investigation; and I will add, that the more comprehensive it is, the more agreeable it will be to me."

Giles promptly took up the challenge, and moved the appointment of a committee to examine the state of the Treasury Department in all its particulars. Pending action by the House, a new complication was introduced, which, though meant as a blow at Hamilton, resulted in a signal triumph for him. His enemies got hold of a discharged clerk of the Treasury Department by means of whom they now tried to counteract the effect of Hamilton's challenge. Two days after Hamilton's letter to the Speaker, a memorial from Andrew G. Fraunces was laid before the House making charges which amounted to this: that there was a combination between Hamilton and other officers of the Treasury Department to evade payment of warrants so that they could be bought up for speculative purposes. Hamilton's request for an investigation was allowed to lie on the table, but the memorial from Fraunces was referred to a select committee of which Giles was a member. This circumstance turned out to be much to Hamilton's advantage. Giles was an erect, bold, manly foe; he could not stomach the sort of testimony upon which depended the charges against Hamilton's personal integrity, and he concurred in a report on Hamilton finding that the evidence was "fully sufficient to justify his conduct; and that in the whole course of this transaction the Secretary and other officers of the Treasury have acted a meritorious part towards the public."

Giles, while exonerating Hamilton of the charge of dishonesty, did not desist from pressing his motion for further investigation of the Treasury Department. But he admitted that imputations upon the Secretary's integrity had been quite removed, and he now urged that "the primary object of the resolution is to ascertain the boundaries of discretion and authority between the Legislature and the Treasury Department." In thus shifting his ground he presented a new issue in which the House — and indeed Giles's own party associates — took little interest. The fact was that the attack on Hamilton had failed, that the purpose of showing him to be unworthy of

Washington's confidence had been abandoned as impracticable, and that all that remained was a proposal that the House should again engage in a laborious investigation of the desirability of attempting a new delimitation of the functions of the Treasury Department and of Congress. But this, of course, did not concern Hamilton. He had acted under existing laws and with responsibilities which were defined by them. If Congress saw fit to make new laws, the consequences would fall upon his successor in office, not upon him since he was about to retire. If Congress made fetters for the Secretary, it might even be that some member of Giles's own party would have to wear them. Thus, however Giles's latest proposal might be viewed, it was not attractive. Moreover, it was presented at a time when the House had much more urgent matters to consider. The country was wild with excitement over the retaliating orders and decrees of Great Britain and France, which subjected American interests to injury from both sides. Giles and Page appear to have been the only speakers on the resolution when it was taken up for consideration on February 24, 1794, and both disclaimed any intention of reflecting upon Hamilton. The resolution received decent interment by reference to a committee, with no one objecting. The practical conclusion of the matter was that Hamilton had beaten his enemies once more and beaten them thoroughly.

Before resigning his office, Hamilton added still another great achievement to his record of illustrious service in establishing public authority. The violent agitation against the excise act promoted by the Jeffersonians naturally tended to forcible resistance. One of the counts of Jefferson's indictment of Hamilton's policy which had been presented to Washington was that the excise law was "of odious character . . . committing the authority of the Government in parts where resistance is most probable and coercion least practicable." The parts thus referred to were the mountains of western Pennsylvania. The popular discontent which arose there from the imposition of taxes upon their principal staple — distilled spirits — naturally coalesced with the agitation carried on against Washington's neutrality policy. At a meeting of delegates from the election districts of Allegheny county held at Pittsburgh, resolutions were adopted attributing the policy of the Government "to the pernicious influence of stockholders." This was an echo of

Jefferson's views. But the resolutions went on to declare: "Our minds feel this with so much indignancy, that we are almost ready to wish for a state of revolution and the guillotine of France, for a short space, in order to inflict punishment on the miscreants that enervate and disgrace our Government." This was an echo of the talk in the political clubs that had been formed throughout the country. The original model was apparently the Jacobin club of Paris. The Philadelphia club with which the movement started, soon after Genet's arrival, adopted the Jacobin style of utterance. It declared its object to be the preservation of a freedom whose existence was menaced by a "European confederacy transcendent in power and unparalleled in iniquity," and also by "the pride of wealth and arrogance of power" displayed in the United States. Writing to Governor Lee of Virginia, Washington said that he considered "this insurrection as the first formidable fruit of the Democratic Societies."

Hamilton moved warily, doing whatever lay in his power to smooth the practical working of the system in the hope of "attaining the object of the laws by means short of force." But such was the inflamed state of feeling in western Pennsylvania that no course was acceptable short of abandonment by the Government of efforts to enforce the internal revenue laws. During 1793, there were several outrageous attacks on agents of the Government, and the execution of warrants for the arrest of rioters was refused by local authority. People who showed a disposition to side with the Government had their barns burned. A revenue inspector was tarred and feathered, and was run out of the district. The patience with which the Government endured insults to its authority encouraged the mob spirit. On July 16, 1794, the house of Inspector Neville was attacked by a mob, and, when he appealed to the local authorities for protection, he was notified that there was such a general combination of the people that the laws could not be executed. Neville, a revolutionary veteran of tried valor, was able to obtain the help of an officer and eleven soldiers from Fort Pitt, but the mob was too numerous and too well armed to be withstood by so weak a force. After a skirmish in which the mob fired the buildings and the place became untenable, the troops had to surrender. Soon after this affair, a convention of delegates from the four western counties of Pennsylvania was called to meet on August 14 to concert measures for united action. Organized insurrection had, in fact, begun.

"The Government," said Washington, "could no longer remain a passive spectator of the contempt with which the laws were treated." But when he called for Cabinet opinions, the old variance at once showed itself. Randolph thought that calm consideration of the situation "banishes every idea of calling the militia into immediate action." He pointed out that the disaffected region had more than fifteen thousand white males above the age of sixteen, and that sympathy with the insurgents was active in "several counties in Virginia having a strong militia." There was also the risk that the insurgents might seek British aid, in which case a severance of the Union might result. Randolph also enlarged upon the expense that would attend military operations and questioned whether the funds could be obtained. He advised a proclamation and the appointment of commissioners to treat with the insurgents. Should such means fail, and should it appear that the judiciary authority was withstood, then at last military force might be employed.

Hamilton held that "a competent force of militia should be called forth and employed to suppress the insurrection, and support the civil authority." It appeared to him that "the very existence of the Government demands this course." He urged that the force employed ought "to be an imposing one, such, if practicable, as will deter from opposition, save the effusion of the blood of the citizens, and serve the object to be accomplished." He proposed a force of twelve thousand men, of whom three thousand were to be cavalry, and he advised that, in addition to the Pennsylvania militia, New Jersey, Maryland, and Virginia should each contribute a quota.

All the members of the Cabinet except Randolph concurred in Hamilton's opinion. The practical execution of the measures was entrusted to Hamilton, who acted with great sagacity. Some appearance of timidity and inertia in Pennsylvania state authority was indirectly but effectually counteracted by measures which showed that the military expedition would move even if Pennsylvania held back. Although some troops were to gather at Carlisle, Pennsylvania, others were to meet at Cumberland Fort, Virginia. The business was so shrewdly managed that Pennsylvania state authority fell obediently into line, and the insurgents were so cowed by the determined action of the Government that they submitted without a struggle. Washington thought that this event would react upon the clubs and "effectuate their annihilation sooner than it might otherwise have happened." A general collapse among them certainly followed, and they disappeared from the political scene.

It is in the nature of precaution that the more successful it is the less necessary it appears to have been, and thus the complete success of Hamilton's management furnished his enemies with a new argument against him of which they afterwards made great use. The costly military expedition that had no fighting to do was continually held up to public ridicule. That the expense was trifling in comparison with the objects achieved must deeply impress any one who examines the records of the times. A mistake might have been fatal to the existence of the Government. It has become so powerful and massive since that time, that we can hardly realize what a rickety structure it then was, and how readily, in less capable hands, it might have collapsed.

Randolph, then Secretary of State, seems to have been in a panic. Fauchet, the French minister at that time, reported to his government that Randolph called upon him and with a grief-stricken countenance declared, "It is all over; a civil war is about to ravage our unhappy country." He represented to Fauchet that there were four men whose talents, influence, and energy might save it. "But debtors of English merchants, they will be deprived of their liberty if they take the smallest step." He wanted to know whether Fauchet could lend "funds sufficient to shelter them from English persecution." Fauchet's letter was captured by the British and made public. Randolph's explanations did not clear up the obscurity that surrounds the affair. His version was that the four men were flour merchants who were being pressed by their creditors "and that the money was wanted only for the purpose of paying them what was actually due to them in virtue of existing contracts." Even on his own showing it was a shady transaction, and he retired from Washington's Cabinet under a cloud.

Washington always had difficulty about the composition of his Cabinet. A capable man had been found to succeed Randolph as Attorney-General in the person of William Bradford, an able Pennsylvania lawyer, but he died in 1795, and was succeeded by Charles Lee of Virginia. When

Knox resigned in 1794, the vacancy was filled by transferring to the War Department Timothy Pickering of Massachusetts, who had previously served as Postmaster-General. When Hamilton retired, January, 1795, he was succeeded by Oliver Wolcott of Connecticut, who had been Comptroller of the Treasury. After Randolph has been discredited by the Fauchet letter, the office of Secretary of State went a-begging. It was offered to William Patterson of New Jersey, to Thomas Johnson of Maryland, to Charles Cotesworth Pinckney of South Carolina, but all these men declined. Washington got word that Patrick Henry, the old antagonist of the Constitution, was showing Federalist leanings in opposition to Jefferson and Madison, and Henry was then tendered the appointment, but he too declined. Others were approached but all refused, and meanwhile Pickering, though Secretary of War, also attended to the work of the State Department. The matter was finally settled by permanently attaching Pickering to the State Department, while the vacancy thus created at the head of the War Department was filled by James McHenry, an appointment which Washington himself described as "Hobson's choice."

Hamilton, although out of the Cabinet, still remained a trusted adviser, and he rendered splendid service at a dangerous crisis. In spite of the fact that the Jay treaty had been ratified by the Senate in June, 1795, it was an issue in the Fall elections that year. Jefferson held that the treaty was an "execrable thing," an "infamous act, which is really nothing more than a treaty of alliance between England and the Anglo-men of this country against the Legislature and the people of the United States." Giles, who had been in close consultation with Jefferson, moved with characteristic energy to translate Jefferson's views into congressional action.

The Fourth Congress met on December 7, 1795, and although a Federalist, Jonathan Dayton of New Jersey was elected Speaker, the Republicans were strong enough to tone down the reply to the President's address by substituting for an expression of "undiminished confidence" an acknowledgment of "zealous and faithful services," which expressed "approval of his course." On March 24, 1796, the House by a vote of 62 to 37 adopted a resolution calling upon the President to lay before it his instructions to Jay, "together with the correspondence and the other documents relative to said treaty." Advised by Hamilton and sustained by his whole Cabinet, Washington replied on March 30, by declining to comply because concurrence of the House was not necessary to give validity to the treaty, and "because of the necessity of maintaining the boundaries fixed by the Constitution between the different departments." The House retorted by a resolution declaring its right to judge the merits of the case when application was made for an appropriation to give effect to a treaty. Debate on this issue, which is still an open one in our constitutional system, began on April 14 and continued for sixteen days. Madison opposed the execution of the treaty, but the principal speech was made by Giles, whose argument covers twenty-eight columns in the *Annals*. As the struggle proceeded, the Jeffersonians lost ground. It became evident that weighty elements of public opinion were veering around to the support of the treaty as the best arrangement attainable in the circumstances. The balance of strength became so close that the scales were probably turned by a speech of wonderful power and eloquence delivered by Fisher Ames. A decision was reached on April 30, the test question being on declaring the treaty "highly objection-

WASHINGTON AND HIS COLLEAGUES

able." Forty-eight votes were cast on each side and the Speaker gave his decision for the negative. In the end, the House stood 51 to 48 in favor of carrying the treaty into effect. Only four votes for the treaty came from the section south of Mason and Dixon's line.

During the agitation over the Jay treaty the rage of party spirit turned full against Washington himself. He was blackguarded and abused in every possible way. He was accused of having shown incapacity while General and of having embezzled public funds while President. He was nicknamed "the Step-Father of his country." The imputation on his honor stung so keenly that he declared "he would rather be in his grave than in the Presidency," and in private correspondence he complained that he had been assailed "in terms so exaggerated and indecent as could scarcely be applied to a Nero, a notorious defaulter, or even to a common pickpocket." The only rejoinder which his dignity permitted him to make is that contained in his Farewell Address, dated September 17, 1796, in which he made a modest estimate of his services and made a last affectionate appeal to the people whom he had so faithfully served.

PARTY VIOLENCE 193

The Farewell Address was not a communication to Congress. It was issued in view of the approaching presidential election, to give public notice that he declined "being considered among the number of those out of whom a choice is to be made." The usual address to Congress was delivered by Washington on December 7, 1796, shortly after the opening of the second session of the Fourth Congress. The occasion was connected in the public mind with his recent valedictory, and Congress was ready to vote a reply of particularly cordial tenor. Giles stood to his guns to the last, speaking and voting against complimentary resolutions. "He hoped gentlemen would compliment the President privately, as individuals; at the same time, he hoped such adulation would never pervade the House." He held that "the Administration has been neither wise nor firm," and he acknowledged that he was "one of those who do not think so much of the President as some others do." On this issue Madison forsook him, and Giles was voted down, 67 to 12. Among the eleven who stood by Giles was a new member who made his first appearance that session — Andrew Jackson of Tennessee. In later years, when Giles's opinions had been modified by experience and reflection, he regretted his attitude towards Washington. It is due to Giles to say that he did not stab in the dark. He had qualities of character that under better constitutional arrangements would have invigorated the functions of the House as an organ of control, but at that time, with the separation that had been introduced between the House and the Administration, his energy was mischievous and his intrepidity was a misfortune to himself and to his party.

Washington's term dragged to its close like so much slow torture. Others might resign, but he had to stand at his post until the end, and it was a happy day for him when he got his discharge. His elation was so manifest that it was noticed by John Adams. Writing to his wife about the ceremony the day after the inauguration, Adams remarked that Washington "seemed to me to enjoy a triumph over me. Methought I heard him say, 'Ay! I am fairly out, and you fairly in! See which of us will be the happiest.'"

CHAPTER IX

THE PERSONAL RULE OF JOHN ADAMS

THE narrow majority by which John Adams was elected did not accurately reflect the existing state of party strength. The electoral college system, by its nature, was apt to distort the situation. Originally the electors voted for two persons without designating their preference for President. There was no inconvenience on that account while Washington was a candidate, since he was the first choice of all the electors; but in 1796, with Washington out of the field, both parties were in the dilemma that, if they voted solidly for two candidates, the vote of the electoral college would not determine who should be President. To avert this situation, the adherents of a presidential candidate would have to scatter votes meant to have only vice-presidential significance. This explains the wide distribution of votes that characterized the working of the system until it was changed by the Twelfth Amendment adopted in 1804.

In 1796, the electoral college gave votes to thirteen candidates. The Federalist ticket was John Adams and Thomas Pinckney of South Carolina. Hamilton urged equal support of both as the surest way to defeat Jefferson; but eighteen Adams electors in New England withheld votes from Pinckney to make sure that he should not slip in ahead of Adams. Had they not done so, Pinckney would have been chosen President, a possibility which Hamilton foresaw because of Pinckney's popularity in the South. New York, New Jersey, and Delaware voted solidly for Adams and Pinckney as Hamilton had recommended, but South Carolina voted solidly for both Jefferson and Pinckney, and moreover Pinckney received scattering votes elsewhere in the South. The action of the Adams electors in New England defeated Pinckney, and gave Jefferson the vice-presidency, the vote for the leading candidates being 71 for Adams, 68 for Jefferson, and 59 for Pinckney. The tendency of such conditions to inspire political feuds and to foster factional animosity is quite obvious. This situation must be borne in mind, in order to make intelligible the course of Adams's administration.

Adams had an inheritance of trouble from the same source which had plagued Washington's administration, — the efforts of revolutionary France to rule the United States. In selecting Monroe to succeed Morris, Washington knew that the former was as friendly to the French Revolution as Morris had been opposed to it, and hence he hoped that Monroe would be able to impart a more friendly feeling to the relations of the two countries. Monroe arrived in Paris just after the fall of Robespierre. The Committee of Public Safety then in possession of the executive authority hesitated to receive him. Monroe wrote to the President of the National Convention then sitting, and a decree was at once passed that the Minister of the United States should "be introduced in the bosom of the Convention." Monroe presented himself on August 15, 1794, and made a glowing address. He descanted upon the trials by which America had won her independence and declared that "France, our ally and friend, and who aided in the contest, has now embarked in the same noble career." The address was received with enthusiasm, the President of the Convention drew Monroe to his bosom in a fraternal embrace; and it was decreed that "the flags of the United States of America shall be joined to those of France, and displayed in the hall of the sittings of the Convention, in sign of the union and eternal fraternity of the two peoples." In compliance with this decree Monroe soon after presented an American flag to the Convention.

When the news of these proceedings reached the State Department, a sharp note was sent to Monroe "to recommend caution lest we be obliged at some time or other to explain away or disavow an excess of fervor, so as to reduce it down to the cool system of neutrality." The French Government regarded the Jay treaty as an affront and as a violation of our treaties with France. Many American vessels were seized and confiscated with their cargoes, and hundreds of American citizens were imprisoned. Washington thought that Monroe was entirely too submissive to such proceedings; therefore, on August 22, 1796, Monroe was recalled and soon after Charles Cotesworth Pinckney was appointed in his stead.

The representation of France in the United States had been as mutable as her politics. Fauchet, who succeeded Genet, retired in June, 1795, and was succeeded by Adet, who like his predecessors, carried on active interference with American

THE PERSONAL RULE OF JOHN ADAMS

politics, and even attempted to affect the presidential election by making public a note addressed to the Secretary of State complaining of the behavior of the Administration. In Adams's opinion this note had some adverse effect in Pennsylvania but no other serious consequences, since it was generally resented. Meanwhile Pinckney arrived in France in December, 1796, and the Directory refused to receive him. He was not even permitted to remain in Paris; but honors were showered upon Monroe as he took his leave. In March, 1797, Adet withdrew, and diplomatic relations between the two countries were entirely suspended. By a decree made two days before Adams took office, the Directory proclaimed as pirates, to be treated without mercy, all Americans found serving on board British vessels, and ordered the seizure of all American vessels not provided with lists of their crews in proper form. Though made under cover of the treaty of 1778, this latter provision ran counter to its spirit and purpose. Captures of American ships began at once. As Joel Barlow wrote, the decree of March 2, 1797, "was meant to be little short of a declaration of war."

The curious situation which ensued from the

efforts made by Adams to deal with this emergency cannot be understood without reference to his personal peculiarities. He was vain, learned, and self-sufficient, and he had the characteristic defect of pedantry: he overrated intelligence and he underrated character. Hence he was inclined to resent Washington's eminence as being due more to fortune than to merit, and he had for Hamilton an active hatred compounded of wounded vanity and a sense of positive injury. He knew that Hamilton thought slightingly of his political capacity and had worked against his political advancement, and he was too lacking in magnanimity to do justice to Hamilton's motives. His state of mind was well known to the Republican leaders, who hoped to be able to use him. Jefferson wrote to Madison suggesting that "it would be worthy of consideration whether it would not be for the public good to come to a good understanding with him as to his future elections." Jefferson himself called on Adams and showed himself desirous of cordial relations. Mrs. Adams responded by expressions of pleasure at the success of Jefferson, between whom and her husband, she said, there had never been "any public or private animosity." Such rejoicing over the

THE PERSONAL RULE OF JOHN ADAMS 201

defeat of the Federalist candidate for Vice-President did not promote good feeling between the President and the Federalist leaders.

The morning before the inauguration, Adams called on Jefferson and discussed with him the policy to be pursued toward France. The idea had occurred to Adams that a good impression might be made by sending out a mission of extraordinary weight and dignity, and he wanted to know whether Jefferson himself would not be willing to head such a mission. Without checking Adams's friendly overtures, Jefferson soon brought him to agree that it would not be proper for the Vice-President to accept such a post. Adams then proposed that Madison should go. On March 6, Jefferson reported to Adams that Madison would not accept. Then for the first time, according to Adams's own account, he consulted a member of his Cabinet, supposed to be Wolcott although the name is not mentioned.

Adams took over Washington's Cabinet as it was finally constituted after the retirement of Jefferson and Hamilton and the virtual expulsion of Randolph. The process of change had made it entirely Federalist in its political complexion, and entirely devoted to Washington and Hamilton in its personal sympathies. That Adams should have adopted it as his own Cabinet has been generally regarded as a blunder, but it was a natural step for him to take. To get as capable men to accept the portfolios as those then holding them would have been difficult, so averse had prominent men become to putting themselves in a position to be harried by Congress, with no effective means of explaining and justifying their conduct. Congress then had a prestige which it does not now possess, and its utterances then received consideration not now accorded. Whenever presidential electors were voted for directly by the people, the poll was small compared with the vote for members of Congress. Moreover, there was then a feeling that the Cabinet should be regarded as a bureaucracy, and for a long period this conception tended to give remarkable permanence to its composition.

When the personal attachments of the Cabinet chiefs are considered, it is easy to imagine the dismay and consternation produced by the dealings of Adams with Jefferson. By the time Adams consulted the members of his Cabinet, they had become suspicious of his motives and distrustful of his character. Before long they were writing to Washington and Hamilton for advice, and were endeavoring to manage Adams by concerted action. In this course they had the cordial approval of leading Federalists, who would write privately to members of the Cabinet and give counsel as to procedure. Wolcott, a Federalist leader in Connecticut, warned his son, the Secretary of the Treasury, that Adams was "a man of great vanity, pretty capricious, of a very moderate share of prudence, and of far less real abilities than he believes himself to possess," so that "it will require a deal of address to render him the service which it will be essential for him to receive."

The policy to be pursued was still unsettled when news came of the insulting rejection of Pinckney and the domineering attitude assumed by France. On March 25, Adams issued a call for the meeting of Congress on May 15, and then set about getting the advice of his Cabinet. He presented a schedule of interrogatories to which he asked written answers. The attitude of the Cabinet was at first hostile to Adams's favorite notion of a special mission, but as Hamilton counseled deference to the President's views, the Cabinet finally approved the project. Adams appointed John Marshall of Virginia and Elbridge Gerry of Massachusetts to serve in conjunction with Pinckney, who had taken refuge in Holland.

Strong support for the Government in taking a firm stand against France was manifested in both Houses of Congress. Hamilton aided Secretary Wolcott in preparing a scheme of taxation by which the revenue could be increased to provide for national defense. With the singular fatality that characterized Federalist party behavior throughout Adams's Administration, however, all the items proposed were abandoned except one for stamp taxes. What had been offered as a scheme whose particulars were justifiable by their relation to the whole was converted into a measure which was traditionally obnoxious in itself, and was now made freshly odious by an appearance of discrimination and partiality. The Federalists did improve their opportunity in the way of general legislation: much needed laws were passed to stop privateering, to protect the ports, and to increase the naval armament; and Adams was placed in a much better position to maintain neutrality than Washington had been. Fear of another outbreak of yellow fever accelerated the work of Congress, and the extra session lasted only a little over three weeks.

Such was the slowness of communication in those

days that, when Congress reassembled at the regular session in November, no decisive news had arrived of the fate of the special mission. Adams with proper prudence thought it would be wise to consider what should be done in case of failure. On January 24, 1798, he addressed to the members of his Cabinet a letter requesting their views. No record is preserved of the replies of the Secretaries of State and of the Treasury. Lee, the Attorney-General, recommended a declaration of war. McHenry, the Secretary of War, offered a series of seven propositions to be recommended to Congress: 1. Permission to merchant ships to arm; 2. The construction of twenty sloops of war; 3. The completion of frigates already authorized; 4. Grant to the President of authority to provide ships of the line, not exceeding ten, "by such means as he may judge best." 5. Suspension of the treaties with France; 6. An army of sixteen thousand men, with provision for twenty thousand more should occasion demand; 7. A loan and an adequate system of taxation.

These recommendations are substantially identical with those made by Hamilton in a letter to Pickering, and the presumption is strong that McHenry's paper is a product of Hamilton's influence, and that it had the concurrence of Pickering and Wolcott. The suggestion that the President should be given discretionary authority in the matter of procuring ships of the line contemplated the possibility of obtaining them by transfer from England, not through formal alliance but as an incident of a coöperation to be arranged by negotiation, whose objects would also include aid in placing a loan and permission for American ships to join British convoys. This feature of McHenry's recommendations could not be carried out. Pickering soon informed Hamilton that the old animosities were still so active "in some breasts" that the plan of coöperation was impracticable.

Meanwhile the composite mission had accomplished nothing except to make clear the actual character of French policy. When the envoys arrived in France, the Directory had found in Napoleon Bonaparte an instrument of power that was stunning Europe by its tremendous blows. That instrument had not yet turned to the reorganization of France herself, and at the time it served the rapacious designs of the Directory. Europe was looted wherever the arms of France prevailed, and the levying of tribute both on public and on private account was the order of the day. Talley-

THE PERSONAL RULE OF JOHN ADAMS 207

rand was the Minister of Foreign Affairs, and he treated the envoys with a mixture of menace and cajolery. It was a part of his tactics to sever the Republican member, Gerry, from his Federalist colleagues. Gerry was weak enough to be caught by Talleyrand's snare, and he was foolish enough to attribute the remonstrances of his colleagues to vanity. "They were wounded," he wrote, "by the manner in which they had been treated by the Government of France, and the difference which had been used in respect to me." Gerry's conduct served to weaken and delay the negotiations, but he eventually united with his colleagues in a detailed report to the State Department, which was transmitted to Congress by the President on April 3, 1798. In the original the names of the French officials concerned were written at full length in the Department cipher. In making a copy for Congress, Secretary Pickering substituted for the names the terminal letters of the alphabet, and hence the report has passed into history as the X. Y. Z. dispatches.

The story, in brief, was that on arriving in Paris the envoys called on Talleyrand, who said that he was busy at that very time on a report to the Directory on American affairs, and in a few days would let them know how matters stood. A few days later they received notice through Talleyrand's secretary that the Directory was greatly exasperated by expressions used in President Adams's address to Congress, that the envoys would probably not be received until further conference, and that persons might be appointed to treat with them. A few more days elapsed, and then three persons presented themselves as coming from Talleyrand. They were Hottinguer, Bellamy, and Hauteval, designated as X. Y. Z. in the communication to Congress. They said that a friendly reception by the Directory could not be obtained unless the United States would assist France by a loan, and that "a sum of money was required for the pocket of the Directory and Ministers, which would be at the disposal of M. Talleyrand." This "douceur to the Directory," amounting to approximately $240,000, was urged with great persistence as an indispensable condition of friendly relations. The envoys temporized and pointed out that their Government would have to be consulted on the matter of the loan. The wariness of the envoys made Talleyrand's agents the more insistent about getting the "douceur." At one of the interviews Hottinguer exclaimed:—

THE PERSONAL RULE OF JOHN ADAMS 209

"Gentlemen, you do not speak to the point; it is money; it is expected that you will offer money." The envoys replied that on this point their answer had already been given. "'No,' said he, 'you have not: what is your answer?' We replied, 'It is no; no; not a sixpence.'" This part of the envoys' report soon received legendary embellishment, and in innumerable stump speeches it rang out as, "Not one cent for tribute; millions for defense!"

The publication of the X. Y. Z. dispatches sent rolling through the country a wave of patriotic feeling before which the Republican leaders quailed and which swept away many of their followers. Jefferson held that the French Government ought not to be held responsible for "the turpitude of swindlers," and he steadfastly opposed any action looking to the use of force to maintain American rights. Some of the Republican members of Congress, however, went over to the Federalist side, and Jefferson's party was presently reduced to a feeble and dispirited minority. Loyal addresses rained upon Adams. There appeared a new national song, *Hail Columbia*, which was sung all over the land and which was established in lasting popularity. Among its well-known lines is an exulting stanza beginning:

> "Behold the chief who now commands,
> Once more to serve his country stands."

This is an allusion to the fact that Washington had left his retirement to take charge of the national forces. The envoys had been threatened that, unless they submitted to the French demands, the American Republic might share the fate of the Republic of Venice. The response of Congress was to vote money to complete the frigates, the *United States*, the *Constitution*, and the *Constellation*, work on which had been suspended when the Algerine troubles subsided; and further, to authorize the construction or purchase of twelve additional vessels. For the management of this force, the Navy Department was created by the Act of April 30, 1798. By an Act of May 28, the President was authorized to raise a military force of ten thousand men, the commander of which should have the services of "a suitable number of major-generals." On July 7, the treaties with France that had so long vexed the United States were abrogated.

The operations of the Navy Department soon showed that American sailors were quite able and willing to defend the nation if they were allowed the opportunity. In December, 1798, the Navy

Department worked out a plan of operations in the enemy's waters. To repress the depredations of the French privateers in the West Indies, a squadron commanded by Captain John Barry was sent to cruise to the windward of St. Kitts as far south as Barbados, and it made numerous captures. A squadron under Captain Thomas Truxtun cruised in the vicinity of Porto Rico. The flagship was the frigate *Constellation*, which on February 9, 1799, encountered the French frigate, *L'Insurgente*, and made it strike its flag after an action lasting only an hour and seventeen minutes. The French captain fought well, but he was put at a disadvantage by losing his topmast at the opening of the engagement, so that Captain Truxtun was able to take a raking position. The American loss was only one killed and three wounded, while *L'Insurgente* had twenty-nine killed and forty-one wounded. On February 1, 1800, the *Constellation* fought the heavy French frigate *Vengeance* from about eight o'clock in the evening until after midnight, when the *Vengeance* lay completely silenced and apparently helpless. But the rigging and spars of the *Constellation* had been so badly cut up that the mainmast fell, and before the wreck could be cleared away the *Vengeance* was able to make her escape. During the two years and a half in which hostilities continued, the little navy of the United States captured eighty-five armed French vessels, nearly all privateers. Only one American war vessel was taken by the enemy, and that one had been originally a captured French vessel. The value of the protection thus extended to American trade is attested by the increase of exports from $57,000,000 in 1797 to $78,665,528 in 1799. Revenue from imports increased from $6,000,000 in 1797 to $9,080,932 in 1800.

The creation of an army, however, was attended by personal disagreements that eventually wrecked the Administration. Without waiting to hear from Washington as to his views, Adams nominated him for the command and then tried to overrule his arrangements. The notion that Washington could be hustled into a false position was a strange blunder to be made by anyone who knew him. He set forth his views and made his stipulations with his customary precision, in letters to Secretary McHenry, who had been instructed by Adams to obtain Washington's advice as to the list of officers. Washington recommended as major-generals, Hamilton, C. C. Pinckney, and Knox, in that order of rank. Adams made some demur to

THE PERSONAL RULE OF JOHN ADAMS 213

the preference shown for Hamilton, but McHenry showed him Washington's letter and argued the matter so persistently that Adams finally sent the nominations to the Senate in the same order as Washington had requested. Confirmation promptly followed, and a few days later Adams departed for his home at Quincy, Massachusetts, without notice to his Cabinet. It soon appeared that he was in the sulks. When McHenry wrote to him about proceeding with the organization of the army, he replied that he was willing provided Knox's precedence was acknowledged, and he added that the five New England States would not patiently submit to the humiliation of having Knox's claim disregarded.

From August 4 to October 13, wrangling over this matter went on. The members of the Cabinet were in a difficult position. It was their understanding that Washington's stipulations had been accepted, but the President now proposed a different arrangement. Pickering and McHenry wrote to Washington explaining the situation in detail. News of the differences between Adams and Washington of course soon got about and caused a great buzz in political circles. Adams became angry over the opposition he was meeting, and on

August 29 he wrote to McHenry that "there has been too much intrigue in this business, both with General Washington and with me"; that it might as well be understood that in any event he would have the last say, "and I shall then determine it exactly as I should now, Knox, Pinckney, and Hamilton." Washington stood firm and, on September 25, wrote to the President demanding "that he might know at once and precisely what he had to expect." In reply Adams said that he had signed the three commissions on the same day in the hope "that an amicable adjustment or acquiescence might take place among the gentlemen themselves." But should this hope be disappointed, "and controversies shall arise, they will of course be submitted to you as commander-in-chief."

Adams, of course, knew quite well that such matters did not settle themselves, but he seems to have imagined that all he had to do was to sit tight and that matters would have to come his way. The tricky and shuffling behavior to which he descended would be unbelievable of a man of his standing were there not an authentic record made by himself. The suspense finally became so intolerable that the Cabinet acted without consulting the President any longer on the point. The Secretary

THE PERSONAL RULE OF JOHN ADAMS 215

of War submitted to his colleagues all the correspondence in the case and asked their advice. The Secretaries of State, of the Treasury, and of the Navy made a joint reply declaring "the only inference which we can draw from the facts before stated, is, that the President consents to the arrangement of rank as proposed by General Washington," and that therefore "the Secretary of War ought to transmit the commissions, and inform the generals that in his opinion the rank is definitely settled according to the original arrangement." This was done; but Knox declined an appointment ranking him below Hamilton and Pinckney. Thus, Adams despite his obstinacy, was completely baffled, and a bitter feud between him and his Cabinet was added to the causes now at work to destroy the Federalist party.

The Federalist military measures were sound and judicious, and the expense, although a subject of bitter denunciation, was really trivial in comparison with the national value of the enhanced respect and consideration obtained for American interests. But these measures were followed by imprudent acts for regulating domestic politics. By the Act of June 18, 1798, the period of residence required before an alien could be admitted to

American citizenship was raised from five years to fourteen. By the Act of June 25, 1798, the efficacy of which was limited to two years, the President might send out of the country "such aliens as he shall judge dangerous to the peace and safety of the United States, or shall have reasonable grounds to suspect are concerned in any treasonable or secret machinations against the government thereof." The state of public opinion might then have sanctioned these measures had they stood alone, but they were connected with another which proved to be the weight that pulled them all down. By the Act of July 14, 1798, it was made a crime to write or publish "any false, scandalous, and malicious" statements about the President or either House of Congress, to bring them "into contempt or disrepute," or to "stir up sedition within the United States."

There were plenty of precedents in English history for legislation of such character. Robust examples of it were supplied in England at that very time. There were also strong colonial precedents. According to Secretary Wolcott, the sedition law was "merely a copy from a statute of Virginia in October, 1776." But a revolutionary Whig measure aimed at Tories was a very different thing in its practical aspect from the same measure used by a national party against a constitutional opposition. Hamilton regarded such legislation as impolitic, and, on hearing of the sedition bill, he wrote a protesting letter, saying, "Let us not establish tyranny. Energy is a very different thing from violence."

But in general the Federalist leaders were so carried away by the excitement of the times that they could not practice moderation. Their zealotry was sustained by political theories which made no distinction between partisanship and sedition. The constitutional function of partisanship was discerned and stated by Burke in 1770, but his definition of it, as a joint endeavor to promote the national interest upon some particular principle, was scouted at the time and was not allowed until long after. The prevailing idea in Washington's time, both in England and America, was that partisanship was inherently pernicious and ought to be suppressed. Washington's *Farewell Address* warned the people "in the most solemn manner against the baneful effects of the spirit of party." The idea then was that government was wholly the affair of constituted authority, and that it was improper for political activity to surpass the appointed bounds. Newspaper criticism and partisan oratory were among the things in Washington's mind when he censured all attempts "to direct, control, counteract, or awe the regular deliberation and action of the constituted authorities." Hence judges thought it within their province to denounce political agitators when charging a grand jury. Chief Justice Ellsworth, in a charge delivered in Massachusetts, denounced "the French system-mongers, from the quintumvirate at Paris to the Vice-President and minority in Congress, as apostles of atheism and anarchy, bloodshed, and plunder." In charges delivered in western Pennsylvania, Judge Addison dealt with such subjects as Jealousy of Administration and Government, and the Horrors of Revolution. Washington, then in private life, was so pleased with the series that he sent a copy to friends for circulation.

Convictions under the sedition law were few, but there were enough of them to cause great alarm. A Jerseyman, who had expressed a wish that the wad of a cannon, fired as a salute to the President, had hit him on the rear bulge of his breeches, was fined $100. Matthew Lyon of Vermont, while canvassing for reëlection to Congress, charged the President with "unbounded thirst for ridiculous

THE PERSONAL RULE OF JOHN ADAMS

pomp, foolish adulation, and a selfish avarice." This language cost him four months in jail and a fine of $1000. But in general the law did not repress the tendencies at which it was aimed but merely increased them.

The Republicans, too weak to make an effective stand in Congress, tried to interpose state authority. Jefferson drafted the Kentucky Resolutions, adopted by the state legislature in November, 1798. They hold that the Constitution is a compact to which the States are parties, and that "each party has an equal right to judge for itself as well of infractions as of the mode and measure of redress." The alien and sedition laws were denounced, and steps were proposed by which protesting States "will concur in declaring these Acts void and of no force, and will each take measures of its own for providing that neither these Acts, nor any others of the general Government, not plainly and intentionally authorized by the Constitution, shall be exercised within their respective territories." The Virginia Resolutions, adopted in December, 1798, were drafted by Madison. They view "the powers of the federal Government as resulting from the compact to which the States are parties," and declare that, if those powers are exceeded, the

States "have the right and are in duty bound to interpose." This doctrine was a vial of woe to American politics until it was cast down and shattered on the battlefield of civil war. It was invented for a partisan purpose, and yet was entirely unnecessary for that purpose.

The Federalist party as then conducted was the exponent of a theory of government that was everywhere decaying. The alien and sedition laws were condemned and discarded by the forces of national politics, and state action was as futile in effect as it was mischievous in principle. It diverted the issue in a way that might have ultimately turned to the advantage of the Federalist party, had it possessed the usual power of adaptation to circumstances. After all, there was no reason inherent in the nature of that party why it should not have perpetuated its organization and repaired its fortunes by learning how to derive authority from public opinion. The needed transformation of character would have been no greater than has often been accomplished in party history. Indeed, there is something abnormal in the complete prostration and eventual extinction of the Federalist party; and the explanation is to be found in the extraordinary character of Adams's administration.

THE PERSONAL RULE OF JOHN ADAMS

It gave such prominence and energy to individual aims and interests that the party was rent to pieces by them.

In communicating the X. Y. Z. dispatches to Congress, Adams declared: "I will never send another Minister to France without assurance that he will be received, respected, and honored, as the representative of a great, free, powerful, and independent nation." But on receiving an authentic though roundabout intimation that a new mission would have a friendly reception, he concluded to dispense with direct assurances, and, without consulting his Cabinet, sent a message to the Senate on February 18, 1799, nominating Murray, then American Minister to Holland, to be Minister to France. This unexpected action stunned the Federalists and delighted the Republicans as it endorsed the position they had always taken that war talk was folly and that France was ready to be friendly if America would treat her fairly. "Had the foulest heart and the ablest head in the world," wrote Senator Sedgwick to Hamilton, "been permitted to select the most embarrassing and ruinous measure, perhaps it would have been precisely the one which has been adopted." Hamilton advised that "the measure must go into effect with the additional idea of a commission of three." The committee of the Senate to whom the nomination was referred made a call upon Adams to inquire his reasons. According to Adams's own account, they informed him that a commission would be more satisfactory to the Senate and to the public. According to Secretary Pickering, Adams was asked to withdraw the nomination and refused, but a few days later, on hearing that the committee intended to report against confirmation, he sent in a message nominating Chief Justice Ellsworth and Patrick Henry, together with Murray, as envoys extraordinary. The Senate, much to Adams's satisfaction, promptly confirmed the nominations, but this was because Hamilton's influence had smoothed the way. Patrick Henry declined, and Governor Davie of North Carolina was substituted. By the time this mission reached France, Napoleon Bonaparte was in power and the envoys were able to make an acceptable settlement of the questions at issue between the two countries. The event came too late to be of service to Adams in his campaign for reëlection, but it was intensely gratifying to his self-esteem.

Some feelers were put forth to ascertain whether Washington could not be induced to be a candidate again, but the idea had hardly developed before all hopes in that quarter were abruptly dashed by his death on December 14, 1799, from a badly treated attack of quinsy. Efforts to substitute some other candidate for Adams proved unavailing, as New England still clung to him on sectional grounds. News of these efforts of course reached Adams and increased his bitterness against Hamilton, whom he regarded as chiefly responsible for them. Adams had a deep spite against members of his Cabinet for the way in which they had foiled him about Hamilton's commission, but for his own convenience in routine matters he had retained them, although debarring them from his confidence. In the spring of 1800 he decided to rid himself of men whom he regarded as "Hamilton's spies." The first to fall was McHenry, whose resignation was demanded on May 5, 1800, after an interview in which — according to McHenry — Adams reproached him with having "biased General Washington to place Hamilton in his list of major-generals before Knox." Pickering refused to resign, and he was dismissed from office on May 12. John Marshall became the Secretary of State, and Samuel Dexter of Massachusetts, Secretary of War. Wolcott retained the Treasury portfolio until the end of the year, when he resigned of his own motion.

The events of the summer of 1800 completed the ruin of the Federalist party. That Adams should have been so indifferent to the good will of his party at a time when he was a candidate for reelection is a remarkable circumstance. A common report among the Federalists was that he was no longer entirely sane. A more likely supposition was that he was influenced by some of the Republican leaders and counted on their political support. In biographies of Gerry it is claimed that he was able to accomplish important results through his influence with Adams. At any rate, Adams gave unrestrained expression to his feelings against Hamilton, and finally Hamilton was aroused to action. On August 1, 1800, he wrote to Adams demanding whether it was true that Adams had "asserted the existence of a British faction in this country" of which Hamilton himself was said to be a leader. Adams did not reply. Hamilton waited until October 1, and then wrote again, affirming "that by whomsoever a charge of the kind mentioned in my former letter, may, at any time, have been made or insinuated against me, it is a base, wicked, and cruel calumny; destitute even

THE PERSONAL RULE OF JOHN ADAMS 225

of a plausible pretext, to excuse the folly, or mask the depravity which must have dictated it."

Hamilton, always sensitive to imputations upon his honor, was not satisfied to allow the matter to rest there. He wrote a detailed account of his relations with Adams, involving an examination of Adams's public conduct and character, which he privately circulated among leading Federalists. It is an able paper, fully displaying Hamilton's power of combining force of argument with dignity of language, but although exhibiting Adams as unfit for his office it advised support of his candidacy. Burr obtained a copy and made such use of parts of it that Hamilton himself had to publish it in full.

In this election the candidate associated with Adams by the Federalists was Charles Cotesworth Pinckney of South Carolina. Though one Adams elector in Rhode Island cut Pinckney, he would still have been elected had the electoral votes of his own State been cast for him as they had been for Thomas Pinckney, four years before; but South Carolina now voted solidly for both Republican candidates. The result of the election was a tie between Jefferson and Burr, each receiving 73 votes, while Adams received 65 and Pinckney 64.

The election was thus thrown into the House, where some of the Federalists entered into an intrigue to give Burr the Presidency instead of Jefferson, but this scheme was defeated largely through Hamilton's influence. He wrote: "If there be a man in this world I ought to hate, it is Jefferson. With Burr I have always been personally well. But the public good must be paramount to every private consideration."

The result of the election was a terrible blow to Adams. His vanity was so hurt that he could not bear to be present at the installation of his successor, and after working almost to the stroke of midnight signing appointments to office for the defeated Federalists, he drove away from Washington in the early morning before the inauguration ceremonies began. Eventually he soothed his self-esteem by associating his own trials and misfortunes with those endured by classical heroes. He wrote that Washington, Hamilton, and Pinckney formed a triumvirate like that of Antony, Octavius, and Lepidus, and "that Cicero was not sacrificed to the vengeance of Antony more egregiously than John Adams was to the unbridled and unbounded ambition of Alexander Hamilton in the American triumvirate."

BIBLIOGRAPHICAL NOTE

ABUNDANT materials are available for the period covered by this work. Chief among them are the Annals of Congress, the State Papers, and the writings of statesmen to be found in any library index under their names. The style maintained by Washington early became a subject of party controversy and to this may be attributed a noticeable variation in accounts given by different authors. For instance, Washington Irving, who as a child witnessed the first inauguration parade, says in his *Life of Washington* that the President's coach "was drawn by a single pair of horses." But the detailed account given in the *New York Packet* of May 1, 1789, the day after the ceremony, says that "the President joined the procession in his carriage and four." The following authorities may be consulted on the point:

B. J. LOSSING, article in *The Independent*, vol. xli, April 25, 1889.

MARTHA J. LAMB, article in *Magazine of American History*, vol. xx, December, 1888.

BIBLIOGRAPHICAL NOTE

For details of official etiquette during Washington's administration, the following may be consulted:

GEORGE WASHINGTON, *Diary*, from 1789 to 1791. Edited by B. J. Lossing (1860).

WILLIAM MACLAY, *Journal*, 1789–1791 (1890).

GEORGE W. P. CUSTIS, *Memoirs of Washington* (1859).

JAMES G. WILSON, *The Memorial History of New York* (1893).

ANNE HOLLINGSWORTH WHARTON, *Martha Washington* (1897).

Works of special importance for their documentary matter and for their exhibition of the personal aspect of events are:

J. C. HAMILTON, *History of the Republic of the United States*, 7 vols. (1860).

H. S. RANDALL, *Life of Thomas Jefferson*, 3 vols. (1858).

GEORGE GIBBS, *Administrations of Washington and John Adams*, 2 vols. (1846).

Some economic aspects of the struggle over Hamilton's financial measures are exhibited by:

CHARLES A. BEARD, *Economic Origins of Jeffersonian Democracy* (1915).

New light has been cast upon Genet's mission, causing a great change in estimates of his character and activi-

BIBLIOGRAPHICAL NOTE

ties, by materials drawn from the French archives by Professor F. J. Turner, and presented in the following articles:

"The Origin of Genet's Projected Attack on Louisiana and the Floridas," *American Historical Review,* vol. iii.
"The Policy of France toward the Mississippi Valley," *American Historical Review,* vol. x.
"The Diplomatic Contest for the Mississippi Valley," *Atlantic Monthly,* vol. xciii.

Further references will be found appended to the articles on *Washington, Hamilton, Jefferson, Madison, Jay,* and *John Adams* in *The Encyclopædia Britannica,* 11th Edition.

INDEX

Adams, John, favors making government impressive through ceremony, 8–9; attitude toward Genet affair, 136; re-elected Vice-president, 178; elected President, 195–96; personal characteristics, 200; relations with Jefferson, 200–01; Cabinet, 201–03; defeat at election of 1800, 226

Addison, Alexander, Judge, 218

Algiers, relations with, 104 *et seq.*; treaty with, 112–13

Alien and Sedition laws, 215 *et seq.*

Ames, Fisher, of Massachusetts, 32–33, 43–44, 55, 62, 81, 90, 101, 110, 154, 191

Bacri, the Jew, 113

Barclay, Thomas, 107

Baldwin, Abraham, of Georgia, 110

Barlow, Joel, 119, 199

Barry, John, Captain, 211

Beard, C. A., *Economic Origins of Jeffersonian Democracy*, 76–77

Benson, Egbert, of New York, 55, 66

Boudinot, Elias, of New Jersey, 33, 38, 55, 65–66

Bradford, William, of Rhode Island, 188

Burke, Edanus, of South Carolina, 67, 68

Burr, Aaron, 226

Butler, Pierce, of South Carolina, 29

Cabinet, President's, a development after Washington's administration, 24–25; status of, 50

Campbell, William, Major, 102–103

Carmichael, William, 144

Church, Edward, U. S. consul at Lisbon, 108

Clark, Abraham, of New Jersey, 110, 152

Clark, George Rogers, 120, 124

Clinton, George, of New York, 178

Constellation, The, ship, 113, 210, 211

Constitution, The, ship, 113, 210

Constitutional amendments adopted, 32

Daily Advertiser, 143

Dauphin, The, ship, 106

Dayton, Jonathan, of New Jersey, 152, 190

Dexter, Samuel, of Massachusetts, 223

District of Columbia, exact site to be selected by the President, 74

Ellsworth, Oliver, of Connecticut, 51, 218

Federal Hall, 12–13

Federalist, 70

Federalist party, 224

Finance, National, Tariff bill, 26–31; debt of United States (1790), 57 Assumption bill, 67

INDEX

Finance—*Continued*
et seq., 169; national bank established, 77; mint established, 77

Fishbourn, Benjamin, 90–91

Fitzsimmons, Thomas, of Pennsylvania, 45–46, 47, 49, 110

France, relations with United States, 115 *et seq.*; treaties of 1778, 120–21; representation in United States, 198-99; special mission to, 201 *et seq.*; treaties abrogated (1798), 210; maritime troubles with, 210–12; second mission to, 222

Fraunces, A. G., 179

Freneau, Philip, editor of *National Gazette*, 138

G e n e t, Edmond, appointed French minister to United States, 115; a trained diplomatist, 115–16; audacious mission, 118–22; reception in United States, 122–24; policy toward Louisiana, 124; argues for treaty rights, 132–33; public opinion for, 136–37; arrest by French Government, 144; success, 140–41; United States becomes his asylum, 144; bibliography, 228–29

Germantown, Proposal to place capital at, 72

Gerry, Elbridge, of Massachusetts, 33 *et seq.*, 55, 203, 207, 224

Giles, W. B., of Virginia, 110–12, 166 *et seq.*, 179–81, 191, 193–94

Grange, The, ship, 123, 133

Grayson, William, of Virginia, 51

Great Britain, lays down contraband regulations, 149–50; retains Western posts in America, 154, 158–59; treaty with (1795), 158–62

Greenville, Treaty of (1795), 102

Gwinnett, Button, 91

Hail Columbia, 209–10

Hamilton, Alexander, personal appearance, 3; aid in finance sought by Washington, 4; advises Washington as to deportment, 7–8, 10; appointed Secretary of Treasury, 22–23; rivalry between Madison and, 48; opinion as to establishment of courts, 52; report to Congress (1790), 54 *et seq.*; stand on the question of security of transfer, 64; interest in site for national capital, 71–72; report on manufactures, 77; appreciation of, 78–79; author of interrogatories to the cabinet (1793), 126–128; opinion on French treaty obligations, 131–32; stands against Jefferson, 136; calmness in regard to Genet affair, 137; "Pacificus," 139; "No Jacobin," 143; resigns as Secretary of Treasury (1793), 164–65; party warfare against, 168 *et seq.*; requests a Treasury investigation, 179; opinion as to enforcing law, 185–86; remains trusted adviser, 190–91; aids Wolcott in preparing scheme of taxation, 204; appointed major-general, 212–13; relations with Adams, 224–25; bibliography, 228

Hammond, George, British minister to United States, 150, 154

Hancock, John, 92

Harmar, Josiah, Lieutenant-Colonel, 93, 97

Hazard, Ebenezer, Postmaster-General, 21–22

Henry, Patrick, 189

Humphreys, David, Colonel, 107–08

Indian troubles in the West, 83–87, 93–96, 97–98, 101–02

INDEX 233

Jackson, Andrew, 193
Jackson, James, of Georgia, 53, 60
Jay, John, Secretary of Foreign Affairs, 21; appointed envoy extraordinary to Great Britain (1794), 155-56; mission to England, 158 *et seq.*; elected Governor of New York, 163
Jay treaty, terms of, 158-63; agitation over, 190-92; French attitude toward, 198
Jefferson, Thomas, appointed Secretary of State, 23; attitude on question of assumption of state debts, 73-74; importance of public service, 74; report on the Algerine question, 105-06; as minister to Paris, 117; opinion on French treaty obligations, 129-31, 134-37; "The Anas," 137; disturbs the administration, 138-39; resigns as Secretary of State (1793), 148; for the principle "free ships, free goods," 150; opponent of Hamilton, 174-76; drafts Kentucky Resolutions (1798), 219; elected President, 225-26; bibliography, 228
Johnson, Thomas, of Maryland, 189
Jones, John Paul, Admiral, 107
Judiciary, Establishment of the, 51-53

Kentucky Resolutions, 219
Knox, Henry, Secretary of War since 1785, 21; Secretary of War and of the Navy, 23; submits plan for militia, 82; supports Hamilton in question of treaty obligations, 129-30, 136; recommended as major-general by Washington, 212; question of precedence of rank, 213-14; declines appointment, 215

La Carmagnole, ship, 141
L'Ambuscade, ship, 123-24, 133
L'Ami de la Point à Petre, ship, 141
La Montagne, ship, 141
L'Amour de la Liberté, ship, 141
La Vengeance, ship, 141
Le Cassius, ship, 141
Le Citoyen Genet, ship, 141
Lee, Arthur, 22
Lee, Charles, of Virginia, 188, 205
Lee, R. H., of Virginia, 51
l'Enfant, P. C., 12
Le Petit Démocrate, ship, 141, 142, 143
L'Espérance, ship, 141
Le Vainqueur de Bastille, ship, 141
Little Sarah, ship, 141
Livermore, Samuel, of New Hampshire, 43, 61, 67-68
Livingston, Walter, 22
Louisiana territory, 119, 124

McGillivray, Alexander, Head chief of the Creeks, 83-87
McHenry, James, of Maryland, 189, 205, 223
McIntosh, Lachlan, 91
Maclay, William, of Pennsylvania, Diary of, 19-20, 60, 69, 70-71, 72, 88-89, 107
Madison, James, coöperates with Hamilton in government organization, 2; personal appearance, 3; introduces scheme for raising revenue, 26-31; upholds President's power of removal, 40-41; acts as advisor to Washington, 47; opinion as to system of federal courts, 52; stand on question of security of transfer, 65, 66-67; opinion on creation of a navy, 109-10; "Helvidius," 140; attitude toward non-intercourse, 154; drafts Virginia Resolutions (1798), 219
Marshall, John, opinion on neutrality of United States (1793),

INDEX

Marshall—*Continued*
126; appointed commissioner to France, 203; becomes Secretary of State, 223

Military preparedness, Policy of, 81-83, 96-97, 100-01, 151-52

Monroe, James, 197-98

Morris, Gouverneur, 117-18

Morris, Robert, 4, 29, 35, 72

Moultrie, William, General, 122-23

Murray, W. V., Minister to Holland, 221

Napoleon Bonaparte, 206

National Gazette, 142-43

Naval policy of the United States, 109 *et seq.*

Neutrality, Question of (1793), 125 *et seq.*

New York, desires to be capital of nation, 12; Washington's home in, 15

Nicholas, W. C., of Virginia, 110

Non-intercourse bill, 153-54

North Carolina admitted to the Union (1789), 93

O'Brien Richard, Captain, 106, 108, 109

O'Fallon, James, Dr., 119

Osgood, Samuel, Postmaster-General, 22, 23

Page, John, of Virginia, 42, 61-62

Paine, Thomas, 119

Patterson, William, of New Jersey, 189

Philadelphia club, 183

Pickering, Timothy of Massachusetts, 189, 223

Pinckney, C. C., 189, 198-99, 212-13, 225

Pinckney, Thomas, 145, 148, 150, 155, 196

President of the United States, social position and duties, 5-10; official title, 10-11; power of removal by, 34, 39-42, 89

Putnam, Rufus, General 81

Randolph, Edmund, appointed Attorney-General, 23; opinion on question of French treaty obligations, 129-30; divides influence between factions in cabinet, 136; transferred to State Department, 168; letter to Washington, 177; opinion as to enforcing law, 185; applies to French minister for funds, 187-88; retires, 188

Republican party, 173

Residence act, 74

Rhode Island admitted to the Union (1790), 93

St. Clair, Arthur, General, 97, 98, 100

Sans Pareil, ship, 141

Sedgwick, Theodore, of Massachusetts, 45, 151, 152

Senate, privy council function of, 87-89

Short, William, 144

Smith, Samuel, of Maryland, 110

Smith, William, of South Carolina, 112

Spain, Treaty with (1795), 145-46

Stone, M. J., of Maryland, 68

Story, Joseph, Justice, 50

Talleyrand, 206-09

Tariff, *see* Finance.

Taylor, John, 76

Treasury Department, established by Congress, 34-39; rights and duties of Secretary defined, 42-51; Secretary's report, 55-56

Trenton, proposal to place capital at, 72

Truxtun, Thomas, Captain, 211

INDEX

United States, The, ship, 113, 210

Virginia Resolutions, 219–20

Wadsworth, Jeremiah, of Connecticut, 37
War Department, Opposition to, 81
Washington, George, reluctant to reassume public responsibilities, 1; installed as President (1789), 2; personal characteristics, 5; his magnificence, 13–14; his levees, 18; first message to Congress, 20–21; first cabinet, 22–23; message to Senate (1789), 81–82; differences with the Senate, 87–91; tours, 91–93; church-going habits, 92–93; receives news of St. Clair's defeat, 98–100; concern about Genet affair, 137–38; opinion as to validity of French treaty, 147; dependence upon Hamilton, 147–48; address of Dec. 3, 1793, 150–51; reëlected President, 177–78; party spirit against, 192; Farewell Address (1796), 192–93; death (1799), 223; bibliography, 227–28
Washington, Martha, arrival in New York, 16–17; her entertainments, 18–19
Wayne, Anthony, General, 101, 102–03
West Indies, trade with, 160–61, 162–63
Whiskey insurrection, 182 *et seq.*
White, Alexander, of Virginia, 39
Willett, Marinus, Colonel, 85
Wolcott, Oliver, of Connecticut, 189, 203, 223–24

"X. Y. Z." dispatches, 207–09, 221

AN OUTLINE OF THE PLAN OF THE CHRONICLES OF AMERICA

The fifty titles of the Series fall into eight topical sequences or groups, each with a dominant theme of its own—

I. *The Morning of America*
TIME: 1492-1763

THE theme of the first sequence is the struggle of nations for the possession of the New World. The mariners of four European kingdoms—Spain, Portugal, France, and England—are intent upon the discovery of a new route to Asia. They come upon the American continent which blocks the way. Spain plants colonies in the south, lured by gold. France, in pursuit of the fur trade, plants colonies in the north. Englishmen, in search of homes and of a wider freedom, occupy the Atlantic seaboard. These Englishmen come in time to need the land into which the French have penetrated by way of the St. Lawrence and the Great Lakes, and a mighty struggle between the two nations takes place in the wilderness, ending in the expulsion of the French. This sequence comprises ten volumes:

1. THE RED MAN'S CONTINENT, *by Ellsworth Huntington*
2. THE SPANISH CONQUERORS, *by Irving Berdine Richman*
3. ELIZABETHAN SEA-DOGS, *by William Wood*
4. CRUSADERS OF NEW FRANCE, *by William Bennett Munro*
5. PIONEERS OF THE OLD SOUTH, *by Mary Johnston*
6. THE FATHERS OF NEW ENGLAND, *by Charles M. Andrews*
7. DUTCH AND ENGLISH ON THE HUDSON, *by Maud Wilder Goodwin*
8. THE QUAKER COLONIES, *by Sydney G. Fisher*
9. COLONIAL FOLKWAYS, *by Charles M. Andrews*
10. THE CONQUEST OF NEW FRANCE, *by George M. Wrong*

II. *The Winning of Independence*
TIME: 1763-1815

The French peril has passed, and the great territory between the Alleghanies and the Mississippi is now open to the Englishmen on the seaboard, with no enemy to contest their right of way except the Indian. But the question arises whether these Englishmen in the New World shall submit to political dictation from the King and Parliament of England. To decide this question the War of the Revolution is fought; the Union is born; and the second war with England follows. Seven volumes:

11. THE EVE OF THE REVOLUTION, *by Carl Becker*
12. WASHINGTON AND HIS COMRADES IN ARMS, *by George M. Wrong*
13. THE FATHERS OF THE CONSTITUTION, *by Max Farrand*
14. WASHINGTON AND HIS COLLEAGUES, *by Henry Jones Ford*
15. JEFFERSON AND HIS COLLEAGUES, *by Allen Johnson*
16. JOHN MARSHALL AND THE CONSTITUTION, *by Edward S. Corwin*
17. THE FIGHT FOR A FREE SEA, *by Ralph D. Paine*

III. *The Vision of the West*
TIME: 1750-1890

The theme of the third sequence is the American frontier—the conquest of the continent from the Alleghanies to the Pacific Ocean. The story covers nearly a century and a half, from the first crossing of the Alleghanies by the backwoodsmen of Pennsylvania, Virginia, and the Carolinas (about 1750) to the heyday of the cowboy on the Great Plains in the latter part of the nineteenth century. This is the marvelous tale of the greatest migrations in history, told in nine volumes as follows:

18. PIONEERS OF THE OLD SOUTHWEST, *by Constance Lindsay Skinner*
19. THE OLD NORTHWEST, *by Frederic Austin Ogg*
20. THE REIGN OF ANDREW JACKSON, *by Frederic Austin Ogg*
21. THE PATHS OF INLAND COMMERCE, *by Archer B. Hulbert*
22. ADVENTURERS OF OREGON, *by Constance Lindsay Skinner*
23. THE SPANISH BORDERLANDS, *by Herbert E. Bolton*
24. TEXAS AND THE MEXICAN WAR, *by Nathaniel W. Stephenson*
25. THE FORTY-NINERS, *by Stewart Edward White*
26. THE PASSING OF THE FRONTIER, *by Emerson Hough*

IV. *The Storm of Secession*
TIME: 1830-1876

The curtain rises on the gathering storm of secession. The theme of the fourth sequence is the preservation of the Union, which carries with it the extermination of slavery. Six volumes as follows:

27. THE COTTON KINGDOM, *by William E. Dodd*
28. THE ANTI-SLAVERY CRUSADE, *by Jesse Macy*
29. ABRAHAM LINCOLN AND THE UNION, *by Nathaniel W. Stephenson*
30. THE DAY OF THE CONFEDERACY, *by Nathaniel W. Stephenson*
31. CAPTAINS OF THE CIVIL WAR, *by William Wood*
32. THE SEQUEL OF APPOMATTOX, *by Walter Lynwood Fleming*

V. *The Intellectual Life*

Two volumes follow on the higher national life, telling of the nation's great teachers and interpreters:

33. THE AMERICAN SPIRIT IN EDUCATION, *by Edwin E. Slosson*
34. THE AMERICAN SPIRIT IN LITERATURE, *by Bliss Perry*

VI. *The Epic of Commerce and Industry*

The sixth sequence is devoted to the romance of industry and business, and the dominant theme is the transformation caused by the inflow of immigrants and the development and utilization of mechanics on a great scale. The long age of muscular power has passed, and the era of mechanical power has brought with it a new kind of civilization. Eight volumes:

35. OUR FOREIGNERS, *by Samuel P. Orth*
36. THE OLD MERCHANT MARINE, *by Ralph D. Paine*
37. THE AGE OF INVENTION, *by Holland Thompson*
38. THE RAILROAD BUILDERS, *by John Moody*
39. THE AGE OF BIG BUSINESS, *by Burton J. Hendrick*
40. THE ARMIES OF LABOR, *by Samuel P. Orth*
41. THE MASTERS OF CAPITAL, *by John Moody*
42. THE NEW SOUTH, *by Holland Thompson*

VII. *The Era of World Power*

The seventh sequence carries on the story of government and diplomacy and political expansion from the Reconstruction (1876) to the present day, in six volumes:

43. THE BOSS AND THE MACHINE, *by Samuel P. Orth*
44. THE CLEVELAND ERA, *by Henry Jones Ford*
45. THE AGRARIAN CRUSADE, *by Solon J. Buck*
46. THE PATH OF EMPIRE, *by Carl Russell Fish*
47. THEODORE ROOSEVELT AND HIS TIMES, *by Harold Howland*
48. WOODROW WILSON AND THE WORLD WAR, *by Charles Seymour*

VIII. *Our Neighbors*

Now to round out the story of the continent, the Hispanic peoples on the south and the Canadians on the north are taken up where they were dropped further back in the Series, and these peoples are followed down to the present day:

49. THE CANADIAN DOMINION, *by Oscar D. Skelton*
50. THE HISPANIC NATIONS OF THE NEW WORLD, *by William R. Shepherd*

The Chronicles of America is thus a great synthesis, giving a new projection and a new interpretation of American History. These narratives are works of real scholarship, for every one is written after an exhaustive examination of the sources. Many of them contain new facts; some of them —such as those by Howland, Seymour, and Hough—are founded on intimate personal knowledge. But the originality of the Series lies, not chiefly in new facts, but rather in new ideas and new combinations of old facts.

The General Editor of the Series is Dr. Allen Johnson, Chairman of the Department of History of Yale University, and the entire work has been planned, prepared, and published under the control of the Council's Committee on Publications of Yale University.

Ross & Perry, Inc.
Publishers
216 G Street, N.E.
Washington, D.C. 20002
Telephone: (202) 675-8300
Facsimile: (202) 675-8400

www.ingramcontent.com/pod-product-compliance
Lightning Source LLC
Chambersburg PA
CBHW030240170426
43202CB00007B/61